Alvin Fernald,
Master of
A Thousand Disguises

Books for Young Readers by Clifford B. Hicks

Alvin Fernald, Master of a Thousand Disguises
Alvin Fernald, TV Anchorman
The Wacky World of Alvin Fernald
Alvin's Swap Shop
Alvin Fernald, Superweasel
Alvin Fernald, Mayor for a Day
Alvin's Secret Code
The Marvelous Inventions of Alvin Fernald
Pop and Peter Potts

CLIFFORD B. HICKS

Alvin Fernald, Master of a Thousand Disguises

Illustrated by Eileen Christelow

Holt, Rinehart and Winston | *New York*

Copyright © 1986 by Clifford B. Hicks
Illustrations copyright © 1986 by
Eileen Christelow
All rights reserved, including the right to reproduce
this book or portions thereof in any form.
Published by Holt, Rinehart and Winston,
383 Madison Avenue, New York, New York 10017.
Published simultaneously in Canada by Holt, Rinehart
and Winston of Canada, Limited.

Library of Congress Cataloging in Publication Data
Hicks, Clifford B.
Alvin Fernald, master of a thousand disguises.
Summary: Alvin Fernald, boy detective, combines
his Magnificent Brain with a summer theater's costume
collection to solve a mystery involving hidden
treasure and a secret cave.
[1. Costume—Fiction. 2. Buried treasure—Fiction.
3. Mystery and detective stories] I. Title.
PZ7.H5316Ajm 1986 [Fic] 85-17754
ISBN: 0-03-069628-3

First Edition

Designer: Victoria Hartman
Printed in the United States of America
1 3 5 7 9 10 8 6 4 2

ISBN 0-03-069628-3

For John and Joan—
and our fine years together, though apart

Contents

Alvin Fernald,
Master of
a Thousand Disguises

≈1≈

The First Disguise

"**A**lvin, I have a job for you today."

Alvin Fernald scooped the last bit of Gooey-Flakes cereal into his spoon. He swallowed the cereal and dropped the spoon into the bowl with a clatter.

"But, Mom! It's Saturday. This morning Shoie and I are going fishing, while they're still biting, and this afternoon we're going to work on the tree house, and you know that tonight is Scout meeting, and—"

"That's enough, Alvin. You can do those things after you've put in an hour or two of work for me."

Doggone it! Why do mothers always wait until the last minute to announce in big no-nonsense tones that they have a job for you to do today? Don't they realize that kids make plans, too?

Alvin ran his fingers through his curly orange hair in frustration.

1

He took his cereal bowl and juice glass over to the sink. "How come you aren't making the Pest work today?" The Pest was Alvin's younger sister; he called her that because she was always tagging along after him, trying to do whatever he and Shoie were doing.

"Now, Alvin. Daphne does her share of chores around here. Besides, I think you'll enjoy this job. And Shoie can help if he wants. Daphne, too, for that matter."

"I'll bet you want me to clean the garage. It doesn't *need* it yet, Mom."

"Well, it certainly *does* need it. You left it a mess when you built that thingamajig last week."

"It wasn't a thingamajig. Shoie and I tried to motorize an old wheelchair we found in the dump. We were going to give it to Peanuts Dunkle's little brother, the one with the bad legs, as soon as he's old enough to drive it. That old lawn mower engine worked fine, too, except we didn't gear it quite right, and in our test run Shoie spurted up Oak Street at thirty miles an hour."

"Speaking of your inventions, Alvin, you've got to disconnect that burglar alarm on the door of your room. When I opened the door yesterday to put clean sheets on your bed, that boxing glove came swinging from out of nowhere and hit me on the forehead. I had a headache for hours."

"That burglar alarm is to keep the Pest out of my room, not you."

"Alvin, she knows it's there. She always crawls under it."

"Crawls under it." The words were repeated in a high, little voice as Daphne bounced into the room, golden pigtails swinging in the morning sun. "What are we going to do today, Alvin?"

"Work." The word was a grunt.

"That's right. I want you kids to help me over at the Summer Theater. I've got to make an inventory of everything that's there."

"What's an inventory?" asked Daphne.

"It's just a list. In this case it will be a list of all the costumes that belonged to the theater."

"How come we have to make a list of that old junk?" asked Alvin.

"It's part of my responsibility as secretary-treasurer of the Summer Theater. Unfortunately the theater has gone broke. Too much competition from the movies, television, and the new amusement park, I guess. Anyway, the board of directors wants to sell the costumes to other theaters around the country. I have to prepare a list of costumes so we'll know what we have for sale."

"And you want us to make the list?"

"Yes. I'll get you started. Then I have to go to the Hospital Guild meeting."

"We should be able to write that old list in ten minutes." Alvin headed for the phone. He'd get Shoie to help. They'd go fishing afterward.

"Alvin."

"Yes, Mom?"

"Alvin, I swear your mind—what you and Shoie call your Magnificent Brain—is off dreaming of how to build new thingamajigs all the time. Take a look at your shoes."

Alvin looked down. He was wearing one bedroom slipper and one rubber boot.

·　　·　　·

Shoie arrived while the Pest was eating her breakfast. He was almost a head taller than Alvin, and he bounced on the balls of his feet as he walked. He was known as the Greatest Athlete in Roosevelt School, and took great pride in the title.

As soon as the dishes were done, Mom got a pad of paper and some pencils and headed for the front door. "It's such a nice fall morning, let's walk."

Alvin groaned.

Shoie slipped through the door and did three cartwheels across the lawn. Daphne tried to imitate him, lost control, and crashed into a rosebush. She recovered quickly, before her mother noticed.

At the corner of Maple and Main streets, Mr. Beadle was walking his dog. When he spotted Alvin approaching, he hurried across the street and disappeared around the corner.

Daphne smiled up at Alvin. "I know why he did that."

"Why?"

"Because of what happened the night you tried to be the Human Cannonball."

It was true. In a huge slingshot, propelled by six truck inner tubes, Alvin had shot right across Shoie's trampoline, his intended target, sailed over Mr. Beadle's private hedge, and landed on the soft ground less than six feet from where Mr. Beadle was reading his evening paper on the front porch. From that moment Mr. Beadle had put as much distance as possible between himself and Alvin.

Alvin Fernald had that kind of reputation among the adults of Riverton.

The Riverton Summer Theater was an old barn on the

edge of town. For many years it had been famous throughout the state. A different play was produced every few
weeks during the summer. Scores of famous actors had
been guest performers. Then a big amusement park had
been built in Centerville, twenty miles away. Gradually
the attendance at the theater had dropped off. Now the
Riverton Summer Theater was dying.

Mom took a key from her purse and opened one of the
two big wide-swinging front doors. The floor, sloping down
to the stage, was covered with row upon row of wooden
benches.

The curtain had been opened for the last time. Except
for a few folding chairs the stage was bare.

Mom led the way down an aisle, up a few steps, and on to
the stage.

Alvin stood there looking out at a vast audience that was
only in his mind. "Now I have you, Captain Hook!" he
shouted. "I AM PETER PAN!"

"Pan . . ." came back the echo.

"Don't do that, Alvin," whispered the Pest. "You scare
me."

Mom led the way across the stage. "The costumes are
stored in a room backstage." Even her voice was subdued.
Ghosts of countless past performances might still live here.

They walked under great backdrops, under curtains
hanging from long ropes. They passed huge canvas frames
stacked against the walls, painted to resemble the doors,
windows, and sidewalls of homes.

Mom opened a door and walked inside. Daphne was at
her heels. She gasped as she entered.

A clothing rod ran along one entire wall. Hanging from it

were hundreds of costumes. Daphne ran over and took one off its hanger. She put a crown on her head, and held a long velvet gown in front of her body. The Pest had been transformed into a princess.

Alvin grabbed a black coat off the rack and slipped into it. Long tails dragged on the floor behind him. From the shelf above the rack he pulled down a stovepipe hat and put it on. It dropped to his nose. "Look at me! I'm Abe Lincoln!"

Each new hanger was a delight. There was an Indian headdress and loincloth, a fireman's helmet, a Southern gentleman's suit that made Shoie look like Colonel Sanders, a black devil's costume complete with pitchfork, even the winged costume of a huge bat.

Daphne screamed aloud when she suddenly discovered the ugly head of a huge gorilla hidden behind a shaggy black suit.

Meanwhile Shoie found a horse's head draped across a hanger. When he tried to pull it off the hanger, he found it connected to a cloth suit that looked like two sets of pajama pants sewn together. "What's this?" he asked.

"That's a horse costume, like they used years ago in burlesque shows," explained Mom. "Put it on, Shoie. Climb into the front legs and put your head up into the horse's head."

Shoie followed her instructions.

Mom then climbed into the rear legs, bent over, and put her hands on Shoie's hips. They both were completely hidden. "Okay, Shoie. Start prancing around."

The horse cavorted around the room, head bouncing,

tail swinging this way and that. It skidded to a stop in front of Alvin and gravely bowed its head. The Pest laughed so hard she went into a coughing fit.

Along another wall of the room was a long mirror with at least a hundred light bulbs around it. There was a counter-top just beneath the mirror. Scattered across it were brushes and combs.

Daphne picked up a tube that looked like toothpaste. "What's this?"

"All the tubes are filled with makeup, dear. And in the drawers beneath the countertop there are wigs, beards, and moustaches."

"Wow!" exclaimed Alvin. "Halloween is only three weeks away. Think of what we can do with all this stuff."

"Now, Alvin. Don't forget that this is still the property of the Summer Theater. You children be very careful with these costumes."

She looked at her watch. "I've got to go to that Hospital Guild meeting. You kids start taking inventory. Just make a list of everything in the room. Describe each item in a few words." She swung out a hanger. "You might call this a 'man's long overcoat.' And this a 'child's short velvet pants.' Do you think you can do that?"

"No sweat, Mom."

As soon as she was gone, the kids again began donning the costumes. Alvin climbed into a pair of velvet pants, pasted a beard across his face, placed a crown around his ears, and proclaimed himself king. Shoie climbed into the gorilla suit and went lumbering across the floor toward the Pest, who recoiled in terror.

Finally Alvin suggested that they go to work on the inventory. The Pest sat down at the makeup counter with a pad of paper. Alvin and Shoie took turns calling out the costumes.

An hour later Daphne's fingers were so cramped she could scarcely write.

"Let's take a break," said Alvin, stretching his arms high above his head. "Let's get some fresh air."

"I'm all for that, old bean," said Shoie.

As he started across the room, Alvin noticed the horse costume lying on a table. "Hey! Let's have some fun with this. Pest, you put on that cheerleader's outfit, and take along the baton. We'll put on a show."

"Maybe we'd better not do that, Alvin. You know what Mom said about taking care of the costumes."

"Oh, c'mon. We won't hurt anything. You be the front half of the horse, Shoie. You've had experience. I'll be the back end of the horse."

"You've had experience at that, too, old man," offered Shoie.

Alvin pretended he hadn't heard. "Pest, you dress in here. We'll wait until we get outdoors to get inside the horse so we won't stumble on the steps."

Outside, the sun was so bright they were momentarily blinded. They waited for the Pest, who suddenly appeared in a cheerleader's outfit designed for someone twice her size. The short skirt was lost under the bright red sweater, which came to her knees. In her hand she held a baton, and gave it a tentative twirl.

"What's your plan, old man?" asked Shoie.

"No plan at all," Alvin said cheerfully. "Let's just see what happens to a cheerleader and a prancing horse."

Shoie climbed into the front legs and put on the horse's head. "Hey! I sure can't see much out of this little hole up here." His voice was muffled.

"You don't need to see much," said Alvin. He climbed into the rear legs, and put his hands on Shoie's hips. Just below his face there was a circular opening in the costume. It enabled him to see the floor and get fresh air. He rotated his rear end. He could feel the horse's tail swirl behind him.

"Hey, Pest! Lead us down Maple Street," ordered Alvin.

Shoie lurched forward, almost tearing himself from Alvin's grasp. Alvin leaped after him, only to jolt Shoie in the back. They went down in a pile of horse's legs, head over tail. When Alvin tried to stand up, the horse costume trapped him on the ground. When Shoie tried to stand up, the same thing happened.

"Both together," panted Alvin. "One . . . Two . . . Three!" They managed to stagger upright.

"Come on, you guys. Stop horsing around!" Daphne giggled as she realized what she had just said. "Let's parade over past the playground."

Daphne twirled the baton and headed down the street. Shoie scrambled after, catching an occasional glimpse of her through the hole in the horse's neck. Alvin couldn't see a thing except the back of Shoie's legs and his own two Adidas.

He heard the screech of a bicycle coming to a halt,

brakes applied full force. "Hey! Who's in there? What's going on?" Then a peal of laughter that climbed up the scale a full octave. It could only be Peanuts Dunkle's giggle. Peanuts was an old friend of Alvin's who had the biggest collection of live garter snakes in town—a collection that had won him a blue ribbon at the last Riverton Hobby Fair.

Shoie trotted several steps to the right; Alvin, of course, followed.

"Ladies and gentlemen! Come watch Oscar the Performing Horse." Daphne's voice was high and loud.

Alvin heard the shuffling of several feet. Into his narrow field of view came two sets of sneakers and a single tiny bare foot. Peanuts giggled again. Shoie nodded his head, and Alvin waggled his tail.

Shoie whispered something that Alvin couldn't hear.

"What?"

"Sit down. Just sit down on the sidewalk."

Alvin did as he was told, sinking his rear end to the ground. Shoie followed, until he was squatting on Alvin's lap. Oscar the horse sat there, resting, nodding his head sleepily. A laugh went up from the hidden crowd. Then with a gasp Shoie rolled over and laid on the ground. Alvin followed.

Alvin's nose was buried in Shoie's belt. The sweat rolled down his cheeks, and his legs were cramped. He'd had enough. He had to get out of the horse suit before he suffocated.

He removed his arms from Shoie's waist and pushed himself to his feet. At least he tried. Instead he tumbled back down on top of Shoie, with the horse's tail around his neck.

There was a roar of laughter.

Alvin heaved with all his might and managed to poke his head out from under the costume.

"Why, it's Alvin!" shouted Peanuts. "It's Alvin Fernald!"

Alvin grinned up at the crowd of kids and several adults who had gathered to watch the show. Worm Wormley and the Pinkepank sisters were there among others. So was Mr. Beadle with an armful of groceries.

"Yes, it's Alvin Fernald," Alvin said proudly. "Alvin Fernald, Master of a Thousand Disguises."

Mr. Beadle turned and scurried for home.

≈ 2 ≈

Daphne Becomes
a Make-up Artist

"**M**om, would anybody care if Shoie and I spent some more time inside the Summer Theater?" Alvin asked at supper that night.

"Me, too," said the Pest.

Alvin gave his sister a nasty look, then changed it to a sweet smile as his mother glanced across at him.

"I don't know," Mom said doubtfully. "Why do you want to spend time there?"

"I want to master the art of disguise," Alvin announced.

"Me, too," piped up the Pest.

"What do you think, Raymond?" Mom turned to Dad.

Sergeant Fernald of the Riverton Police Department cleared his throat. "I don't think it's a very good idea."

"Why not?" Alvin asked.

"Well, the theater is a public building. And kids shouldn't play unsupervised in public buildings."

"We won't be playing. We'll be *learning*. All about costumes, and makeup, and false beards, and everything like that. Who knows? Maybe someday I'll be a famous actor."

"You already are the best actor I know," Dad said dryly.

"I'll tell you what," said Alvin. "We'll make a deal with you. Sooner or later the theater will sell all those costumes. Then they'll all have to be boxed for shipment. Shoie and I—" he glanced at Daphne "—and the Pest—will do all that work free if you'll let us play around with the stuff until then."

Alvin's mother glanced at her husband. "That's quite an offer, Raymond." She turned back to Alvin. "I'll tell you what I'll do. I'll call Elliott Ebright, the president of the Summer Theater. I'll tell him your offer. If he agrees, then it's all right with me. But if I hear even one complaint, I'll have to call the whole thing off. And when the costumes are sold, you three kids will be responsible for packing them properly for shipment. No arguments from you at that time. Just hard work."

Alvin swallowed his token bite of green beans. Despite the taste of the green beans, he smiled to himself.

He washed out the horrible taste with half a glass of milk. *Let's see. Which disguise should I try first? A clown? A cowboy? A fat man?*

Maybe the gorilla; it sure was scary.

The next morning Daphne was waiting on the library steps when Mrs. Bishop unlocked the front door. They knew each other very well. Whenever Alvin Fernald wanted information, he sent his sister to see Mrs. Bishop. When the Magnificent Brain was in high gear, it couldn't be bothered with learning routine facts. The Pest often fed the Magnificent Brain the information it required to produce one of its miraculous plans.

"Good morning, Daphne. What does Alvin need this time?"

"Makeup."

Mrs. Bishop smiled knowingly, and they went inside. "What kind?"

"Theater. Like costumes, and disguises, and things."

"We have two books on that subject. One more advanced than the other. Which do you want?"

"I'll take them both."

Alvin snapped on the bright make-up lights and sat down on a stool in front of the mirror. He opened one of the books.

Daphne reached over and snatched it out of his hands. "*I'm* going to be the make-up artist," she announced in a voice that had the ring of finality. Usually her voice was high-pitched and weak. But when she was *really* determined to get her way, this special tone came into her voice. Alvin recognized it now, and didn't argue.

"Well, what does the book say to do first?"

Daphne took her time scanning the first few pages. Then she said, "Of course. Everybody knows that. The first step is to apply the base."

"What's the base?" asked Shoie. He was standing just behind Alvin. "Is it like first base, or second base?"

"No, silly. It's just a layer of cold cream." She put down the book and reached for a white jar on the countertop. She opened the jar, scooped out a small glob of the cream, and applied spots of it to Alvin's face. With lithe little fingers she spread it across his nose, cheeks, and forehead. When she got to the underside of Alvin's chin, he giggled.

"Tickles!"

"What's the cold cream for?" asked Shoie.

"It makes a nice, even base for all the rest of the makeup, and makes it possible to wipe off the makeup when you are through playing the part." Daphne took a rag from the countertop and vigorously wiped Alvin's face.

"Hey! You're wiping it all off!"

"That's what you're supposed to do, you nerd. Even when you wipe it as hard as you can, you still leave a thin film of cold cream on the skin."

"What's step number two?"

She referred briefly to the book. "Now I'll apply the foundation."

"Okay. Tell us what the foundation is."

"That's the overall color we're going to make your skin." She looked over the makeup kit in front of her, humming the first few bars of "The Teddy Bears' Picnic."

"The book says greasepaint number five is a good, basic color, so we'll try it." She picked up a stick of greasepaint and daubed it on Alvin's face. Then she smeared the daubs until his entire face was the same color—slightly tanned.

She looked him over critically. Then she referred again to the book. "Now comes the fun."

"What's that?"

"I'm going to age you before your very eyes. Like it shows in these pictures."

Using a much darker shade of greasepaint, she drew lines on Alvin's face. When she had finished, dark streaks ran from his nose around the corners of his mouth, beneath his eyes, and in the hollows of his cheeks. Then with deft fingers she blended these darker areas into the foundation.

Alvin watched in amazement as his face changed in the mirror. "Hey! You're doing it! You're making me look like an old man!"

"Of course I am. But I'm not through yet." She picked up a black pencil and drew two up-and-down lines between his eyes, a series of wavy lines across his forehead, and crinkly lines around his eyes and lips. These, too, she worked into the foundation.

"Close your eyes," she ordered.

She opened a box close by. It was filled with scores of eyeglasses of every imaginable type. After considerable study she chose a pair of glasses with round lenses and very fine wire frames. She slipped the bows over Alvin's ears, then adjusted the glasses so they were halfway down his nose.

"Keep your eyes closed," she ordered.

She walked over to the rack of costumes, and looked up at the shelf of hats above. She couldn't reach the one she wanted, but she was very much in command. "I'll take that one," she said, pointing to a beat-up old felt hat. "Get it for me, Shoie."

Shoie handed her the hat.

"Alvin, you're peeking," she said sweetly as she approached him from behind. He squeezed his eyes shut.

When she put the hat on his head it fell down around his ears. She took it off, wadded up some facial tissue, and inserted it beneath the hatband. She put the hat back on his head, then stepped back and inspected him critically. "Okay. Not bad. You can look now."

Alvin was absolutely astounded at what he saw when he opened his eyes. That was not his own face staring out from under the brim of the beat-up hat. It was the face of a wizened, wrinkled old man.

"It's perfect!" Alvin said in a whisper. "Absolutely perfect. Nobody in the world would know me."

"We've got to find a costume to complete the disguise," said Daphne. "Your sneakers are probably okay, and your jeans, but you need a shabby old coat."

Shoie walked over to the wardrobe. He fumbled his way along the line of garments. "How about this one?" he asked, holding up a coat.

The Pest took it from him and eyed it critically. "That's about what we want, but it looks too big. Try it on."

Alvin slipped into the coat. It hung in loose folds around his chest, but somehow that made him look even older.

"Good," said Daphne. "Just what we need. You look like an old, old man who has lost a lot of weight. But the sleeves are much too long. I'll have to pin them up."

When she had finished, Alvin looked in the mirror. He

couldn't believe that ragged old man was Alvin Fernald. Now he wanted to improve his disguise even more. "Lots of old men limp," he said. He hitched his way across the room. "How's this?"

"No, old man," said Shoie. "It simply won't do. You look like you're *faking* a limp. Like you're acting. You've got to make it look like your feet *really hurt.*" He pushed Alvin down on the stool, and pulled off Alvin's right sneaker. "I'll fix that."

He pulled a Hot Ball from his pocket and unwrapped it. Carefully he inserted the hard little piece of candy between Alvin's last two toes. Then he put the shoe back on and tied it as tightly as he could. "That's for realism," he said. "Now walk across the room."

Alvin took one step and almost fell to his knees. "Ouch! Doggone it, Shoie, that's too much!" Instead of taking off his shoe, though, he hobbled across the room. It was painful, but he learned to make progress in spite of his limp. Suddenly he was an actor again.

"Now I've got to change my voice to complete my disguise." He stood there frowning for a moment. "My name is Albert Fennel," he said. "I live alone in a shanty down by the railroad tracks." His voice was deep, yet it had the quaver of an old man.

"Oh, Alvin, that's just exactly right!" exclaimed the Pest. "No one would ever know you really are Alvin Fernald, instead of old Mr. Albert Fennell."

"Wouldn't they? Let's go find out. Let's see how good this disguise is. Let's go out on the street where everyone can see me. One thing, though. You guys will have to stay out of sight. If any of the other kids see you, they'll know I'm somewhere around." Then he added, in the quavering voice of Albert Fennell, "Come along, children. Let's see if anyone recognizes me."

The wizened old figure of Albert Fennell limped out the door. Eventually he would lead the kids into one of the scariest adventures of their lives.

≈3≈

The Adventures
of Albert Fennell

Albert Fennell limped painfully down Main Street. At the corner of Maple he glanced back. A telltale pigtail peeked out from behind Mr. Linkletter's elm tree.

As he turned up Maple, Worm Wormley came whizzing along on his bike.

Albert Fennell waved a hand, beckoning the boy.

Worm slammed on his brakes, leaned far to the right, and skidded to a stop three feet away.

"Young man," quavered Mr. Fennell, "can you tell me where Maple Street is?"

Worm looked him over curiously. "You're on Maple Street right now. You looking for some address in particular?" Worm had a loud, high-pitched voice that had won him first place in the annual Roosevelt School Yelling Contest. He had let out a shriek on the city hall steps that had been heard all the way out on Route 64.

Alvin coughed weakly—a dry hacking sound—and said the first thing that came into his mind. "Two-eighteen. That's what I'm looking for. Two-eighteen Maple Street."

"Lemme think." Worm took off his baseball cap and scratched his head. "That's about two blocks down the street, on the right-hand side. Say! That's just about where a friend of mine lives. His name is Alvin Fernald."

Albert Fennell's face broke into a wrinkled smile. "That's it. That's the address I'm looking for, young man."

"Just go two blocks farther on. Yellow house. Same side of the street you're on now." A pause. "Haven't I seen you somewhere before, mister?"

"I don't believe so, son. I just arrived, you might say."

"You sure do look familiar. Well, so long." Worm pushed sharply on his right pedal, the rear wheel screeched, and he zoomed off.

Alvin Fernald's right hand clutched Albert Fennell's left hand in a victory salute.

It was at that instant that the idea struck Alvin. It was almost too risky. Did he dare? Well, why not?

Albert Fennell limped painfully down the street. And it *was* painful. That doggone lump of hard candy was wearing a blister between his toes.

As the old man approached the Fernald house he could see Mom weeding the flower bed in the front yard. He let his shoulders sag. It aged him even more, and made him appear more decrepit. He cleared his throat. He limped up the front walk until he was only a few steps from Mom. "Morning, ma'am." His voice was a deep quaver.

Mom straightened up. "Good morning." She looked him over sharply. "Can I help you?"

"Ma'am, I want you to believe that I'm not a beggar. I really am not. But I do need some money for the bus fare to Columbus City. I'm willing to work for it. I'll do almost anything."

"How much do you need?"

"Five dollars."

She examined the frail little figure critically. "I'm afraid there's not much around here you can do. Let me think." Obviously she wanted to help. "Perhaps you can do a bit of cleaning up in the garage. Alvin—that's my son—has what he calls his inventing bench out there. It's always a mess. Maybe you could put some of his things back on the shelves, clean off his bench top, and sweep the floor."

Alvin was furious. A stranger messing around with his valuable things? He wouldn't know where to find anything if that happened. Never!

"What's your name?" she asked kindly.

Alvin straightened up, eyes flashing. "My name is Alvin Fernald," he said in his own voice. "And doggone it, Mom, I wish you wouldn't let some old stranger mess around with the stuff on my inventing bench. You may not believe it, but I know exactly where everything is on that bench, and I won't stand for anyone else touching my stuff!"

Mom's mouth was open. She took one step backward, then another. She held up her hands, as though to protect herself. "Alvin! Is that really you?"

"It's me, Mom. I'm in disguise as an old man named Albert Fennell."

She shook her head in disbelief. "My own son. I didn't even recognize my own son!"

· · · ·

Albert Fennell limped up Main Street toward town, determined to carry on his masquerade. He sensed that Daphne and Shoie were somewhere behind him.

At the corner of First Street, six-year-old Sarah Short was just coming out of her house. Alvin had known her almost from the day she was born. She sauntered down the sidewalk toward him, a lollipop in her hand, long black hair falling around her shoulders.

"Hi," she said. She licked the lollipop. "What's your name?"

"Albert Fennell." Alvin suddenly realized he had used his own voice. Hastily he said in a deeper voice, "What's yours?"

"Sarah. I'm little Sarah Short. I'm not only Sarah Short, but I'm *very* short." She giggled at her own joke. "Why do you walk funny?"

Alvin could stand the pain no more. He sat down on a low wall in front of the house. Slowly, still playing the part of an old man, he took off his right sneaker, then his sock. Carefully he felt between his toes. His fingers found a gooey mess. He withdrew his hand and looked at what remained of the Hot Ball.

"What's that, mister?"

"Candy. A Hot Ball."

"Funny place to keep it." A pause. "Can I have some?"

"No, little lady. I'm afraid this one is ruined." He put on his sock and sneaker, and walked up Main Street, hardly limping at all.

≈ **4** ≈

A Hot Ball in the Eye

Alvin Fernald's real adventure started approximately fifteen minutes later, when he walked slowly down Oak Street still in disguise as old Mr. Albert Fennell. As a matter of fact, it started precisely at 11:16 A.M.

He recalled later that he had just looked at the watch his parents had given him on his twelfth birthday, a watch that told the time, date, day of the week, phase of the moon, best time to fish, and had a built-in stopwatch and alarm clock with a "snooze" setting.

The adventure started in front of 169 Oak Street, which was a small house set well back from the street.

As he glanced up from his watch he saw an attractive young woman come out of the house, lock the door, and start down the front walk toward him.

At exactly that same moment a large copper-colored car

came whirling around the corner and stopped with a screech in front of the house. By chance, Alvin noticed that the car had an Illinois license. Inside the car were two men.

The door flew open and one of the men leaped out, a tall slim man with a black beard that covered his face. The man ran straight past Alvin, approached the young woman, and grabbed for her purse.

Alvin watched in amazement as the two struggled along the sidewalk. The woman obviously was not going to give up her purse without a fight.

Albert Fennell disappeared, and Alvin Fernald leaped toward the man. At the same time he shouted, "Help, Shoie! Help!"

Because he attacked the man from the back, and in the disguise of a wizened little man, the thief had no warning that he was being attacked by a wiry twelve-year-old.

Alvin had forgotten that he held in his hand the remnants of the Hot Ball. He flung his arm around the man's head, and quite by accident the Hot Ball popped into the man's eye.

"YEOOOOWWWWW!"

The man instantly dropped the purse and clutched his face. Tears streamed down his cheek. He staggered toward the car.

It was at that moment that the Greatest Athlete in Roosevelt School entered the battle. He grabbed the man by the shoulders and spun him around. At the same time Daphne sat down on the man's right foot and locked her arms around his knee.

"YEEEOOOOOWWW!"

The man stumbled toward the car, an old man on his back, a Great Athlete on his front, a pigtailed girl on his foot, and a Hot Ball in his right eye.

With a mighty effort the bearded man dislodged Shoie's arm, kicked off the Pest with his other foot, pushed Alvin away, and staggered to the car. The car door slammed, and there was the screech of tires.

Then, suddenly, the car stopped. The man thrust his face out the window, and for the first time Alvin got a good look at him. The bright red remnants of the Hot Ball were flowing down his face into his black beard. He had one hand over his wounded eye, and the other eye was glaring first toward Alvin, then toward the young woman.

"*Don't call the police!*" The man spat out each word. "We'll be watching you constantly. *DON'T CALL THE POLICE!*"

Then the car sped around the corner. Alvin caught a glimpse of a heavyset man at the wheel. His large nose looked as though it had been smashed sideways across his face.

For a long moment the three kids and the young lady stood frozen. Then the young lady began weeping silently. Alvin walked over and took her hand in both of his own. He squeezed gently. "Don't cry. It will be all right. He didn't get your purse."

The woman's shoulders shook.

The one thing that Daphne could never stand was to see someone cry. She slipped over and without a word buried her face against the woman's blouse.

At last the woman stopped sobbing. Gently she disengaged Daphne's arms. She opened her purse, took out a handkerchief, and wiped her eyes.

She looked at Alvin. "Thank you. I'm very grateful for your help. It really is a rewarding experience to be saved by a frail little man and two children."

Alvin had forgotten who he was—or who he was supposed to be. "Oh, I'm not a little old man. I'm twelve years old." He cleared his throat. "It's me. Alvin Fernald, Master of a Thousand Disguises."

She looked at him, frowning. "You're not *really* an old man?"

He shook his head. "No. And this is my sister Daphne. And my best friend Shoie."

"I'm so glad to meet you, even if you are in disguise, Alvin. My name is Christina Moller. Come into my house. Let's get acquainted."

The kids looked at each other. Alvin nodded. They followed Christina up the three steps to her porch, and then into her home.

"Sit down, children. Sit down. I'll see if I can find something for us to drink."

Alvin glanced around the room. It was small, but filled with sunlight. On a table next to Alvin's chair was a photograph of a handsome young man, his smiling eyes half-hidden behind a shock of unruly red hair.

Christina walked into the room with four glasses and a large bottle of cola. "Alvin, you're admiring my favorite photograph of my husband Jim. Jim was killed six months ago in a plane crash in South America." There was a moment of silence. "I miss him very much."

"I'm so sorry," said Alvin.

"So sorry," echoed the Pest.

"Well. Let's talk of other things. I trust none of you were hurt by that awful man."

"No," said Alvin. "Can you imagine that guy trying to snatch your purse in Riverton in broad daylight? He should be arrested." He sprang to his feet. "Oh, Christina, I should have told you. Our father—at least the Pest's and my father—well, you know what I mean—is a sergeant on the Riverton Police. If you'll show me your phone I'll call him. He may be able to catch those crooks."

Christina looked at him openly for a moment. "I don't think we should do that. Report this to the police. At least just yet."

"But those guys almost got away with it! That's not good. Just snatching somebody's purse. Why not call the police?"

"The last thing that awful man said to us, in fact the only thing he said, was that they would be watching us constantly, and *not to call the police.* It isn't my fault, but you kids now are involved with two men who could be very dangerous criminals. We can't take any chances with your safety."

"But they tried to steal the money from your purse!" protested Alvin.

"They thought there was something special in the purse, Alvin. Not just money. Something special. Something they were willing to commit a crime to obtain."

"What was it?"

Christina thought for several seconds, her fingers pressing her forehead. "You children deserve to know. And Lord knows, with Jim gone it will be a relief to share my story with someone."

She opened her purse. Reaching inside, she unzipped a compartment along one side and withdrew an envelope. It was a very old envelope, yellowed and brittle. Something had been written on the outside, but the ink had faded with age.

"My story begins with this envelope. No. I take that back. Do you see that clock on the mantel?"

Alvin gazed up at the clock. It was about two feet high. The walnut surfaces gleamed with oil and wax. The old-fashioned gold numerals sparkled in the sunlight. Obviously the clock meant something special to Christina.

"What about the clock?" asked Shoie.

"My story—and the secret within this envelope—begins with that clock."

≈ 5 ≈

In Search of a Grubstake

Alvin settled back in his chair as Christina Moller began her story.

"I don't know whether you kids know anything about your ancestors—your family tree—but I've always been interested in mine. 'Genealogy' is the word that means the study of your ancestors. I suppose you might call me a genealogist. I started tracing my ancestors many years ago. They originally came from Norway and settled in the Midwest.

"But you're probably not interested in any of this. I'm sure you're much more interested in what's of value inside this envelope, and in the mystery of the clock."

"My great-great-grandmother's name was Ada Scheuneman. She was born on a tiny farm in Ohio. When she was seventeen years old she fell madly in love with Tim Martin, a young cabinetmaker who lived in a town nearby."

Daphne's eyes were shining. "Madly in love. How do you know when you're madly in love?"

Christina smiled at her. "You'll know." She glanced at her husband's portrait. "Oh, Daphne, believe me, you'll know."

"Did Tim Martin fall in love with her, too?"

"Oh, indeed. Very much in love. I have many of the love letters they wrote each other over a period of three years. They were desperately anxious to get married, but times were tough in Ohio in the years before the Civil War. There was no money. But there was one way that Tim could express his love for her. He was an artist at working with wood."

"The clock!" exclaimed Alvin, looking up at it.

"Exactly. He put more than a year and a half of his life and his love into that clock. When he finished it, he presented it to her as a special gift. There was a note attached which I still have, though it's so faded and tattered you can scarcely read it. I know every word of it by heart."

"What does it say?" asked Daphne eagerly.

"It says, 'For my beloved Ada. May this clock tick away the minutes, hours, days, and years of our lives together. So long as this clock ticks, so long shall my love for you remain.' "

"Oh, that's so romantic!" exclaimed the Pest.

Alvin, still wearing his old-man's coat, walked over to the fireplace and rubbed his hand over the smooth surface of the clock. "Then Tim married Ada, and became your great-great-grandfather?"

"No. He and Ada never were married."

Tears appeared in the Pest's eyes. "That's so sad. Why didn't they get married?"

"Tim was virtually penniless, and desperate to get what he called a 'grubstake.' That just means enough money to get started. In his case it meant enough money to buy some farmland, some seed, and some livestock, for there was no money in cabinetmaking. With a grubstake he could get married and start raising a family. To get his grubstake, Tim did what many young men did in those days. He headed west to seek his fortune. In his case, he had heard that there was gold to be found in Mexico, so that's where he headed after a tearful farewell to Ada. He promised to write her often, and to return just as soon as he had earned his grubstake, so they could marry."

"Sounds like fun," said Shoie. "I mean, riding off to Mexico to seek your fortune."

"It didn't turn out to be such fun, Shoie. All I know, of course, is what I've read in the letters he wrote to Ada. For the first few months the letters arrived regularly. Tim made his way down through Texas, working at odd jobs, carving small gifts in wood to make enough money for food. He slept under the stars."

Christina paused. "After Tim passed into Mexico, Ada received only two letters from him. One said that times were hard, that he could scarcely get enough to eat. There was no gold and therefore no money to be saved. Then the last letter arrived." Christina's voice dropped. "It said only, 'I have been imprisoned for a crime I did not commit. Don't waste your life on me. There is no chance you will ever see me again.'"

"That's terrible!" exclaimed Daphne. "What a sad, sad story."

"Yes. For six months Ada could scarcely keep control of her mind. She would not leave the house. She was obsessed with polishing the clock. It was a constant reminder that Tim might still be alive. She ate very little, and rapidly lost weight. Then something happened that changed her life."

"What happened?" Alvin was still rubbing his thumb across the surface of the clock.

"One day, as she was sitting in a chair gazing at the clock, it stopped ticking."

There was silence in the room.

It was Daphne who finally whispered, " 'So long as this clock ticks, so long shall my love for you remain.' "

"Had Tim died?" Alvin asked bluntly.

"She thought so. And that was what counted."

≈6≈

Letter from
a Dead Man's Cave

"What did Ada do then?" asked Daphne.

"When the clock stopped, she was convinced that Tim was dead. Within a few days she began showing some signs of normalcy. It had been the uncertainty that almost drove her insane. Now she occasionally smiled. She began going to church regularly.

"One morning her mother noticed that the clock had disappeared from the mantel. She found it hidden under an old quilt in the farthest corner of the attic. That same morning Ada went to town, on her own, and bought a new dress.

"Eventually, at a church supper she met a fine young farmer, poor like Tim, but a good man. Six months later they were married. Thor Gunderson was his name, and he became my great-great-grandfather. They had five children. But they were terribly poor, barely scratching out a living on bad farmland. They both died quite young."

"Did anyone ever find out what happened to Tim?"

"Yes. I found out from Ada's own diary. One day, three years after they were married, while Thor Gunderson was in town buying seed, a stranger rode up to her door. He tipped his hat, and said, 'Morning, ma'am. Is your name Ada Scheuneman?' She nodded her head. 'Then I reckon this letter is for you. It was given to me by a lad over in Indiana, near a town called Riverton. As you can see, it has your name and address on it. Like the lad says in his own note here, he found it in a cave with a dead man. The lad said he hadn't opened the letter, but it might be important.'"

Christina picked up the tattered envelope from the table beside her. "This was the letter the man gave Ada."

It was getting warm in the room. Alvin took off his old-man's coat, and sat down on a footstool. "Read us the letter, Christina," he pleaded. "Don't keep us in suspense."

"Hasn't it occurred to you to wonder how I got my hands on Tim's final letter? Let me explain that first. Then I'll read you the letter.

"I have been able to trace my family back for five generations. My search for my ancestors has taken me all over the country. Two years ago it took me to a distant cousin who is still living in the old family farmhouse in Ohio, a house built before the Civil War. That cousin was able to tell me a lot about Ada Scheuneman, of her passionate love for Tim Martin. She told me of Tim's imprisonment, and of Ada's subsequent marriage. She showed me several of Tim's letters, including his final one which the stranger had delivered to her door. Ada had kept them hidden away in the attic after her marriage. They were tender love letters, exciting to read. They were tied with a slender, faded blue ribbon."

"That's so romantic!" exclaimed Daphne. "I'm going to save all my love letters when I grow up."

Shoie snorted.

"And my cousin led me over to the far corner of the attic. There, covered with an old quilt, was the clock that Tim had made as his love-gift to Ada. We took the clock downstairs and cleaned it. The finish was still in fine shape, and it was as handsome as you see it now.

"When my cousin saw how much I loved the story of Ada and Tim—and my great-great-grandfather Gunderson, too—she suggested that I take the letters for safekeeping. And then, as I was leaving, she said something that meant a great deal to me. 'I want you to have the clock, too,' she said. 'It was the dearest possession of your great-great-grandmother. You are her direct descendant. You should have it.'

"I pretended to resist, but I could hardly wait to get my hands on the clock. It's difficult to express the feeling I have for it. That clock ticks off a love story that spans a century and a half."

≈ 7 ≈

Letter from a Dying Man

"**N**ow can we hear the letter?" asked Alvin impatiently.

Christina pulled the letter from the envelope. She unfolded it with extreme care and laid it on the table beside her. She took her glasses from her purse, put them on, and pushed up on the nosepiece. At last she began to read in a voice so soft the Pest could scarcely hear the words.

" 'My dearest Ada, This letter will tell you how to find a fortune—a fortune much larger than any grubstake we ever dreamed of.

" 'No doubt after three years of absence, and two years without a word from me, you have written me out of your life. You must certainly do just that. My love, I am dying as these words are written.

" 'I am hidden in a small cave in central Indiana near a

town named Riverton. Remember that name, for it will be important to you. There were three bandits. Several miles west of here they waylaid me for whatever coins I might possess. They shot me as I escaped. Despite my wound, I managed to ride several miles, then toppled from my horse. After shooing away my horse, I tumbled down a steep brush-covered embankment, and found myself lying at the mouth of a cave.

" 'I am writing this letter by the sputtering light of my last candle. Even though it is daylight outside it is dark in here. My wound bleeds. I fear I shall die before the candle flickers out. As you no doubt can see, my writing is getting weaker.

" 'The last letter I wrote you was from Juarez. It seems so long ago. I had been imprisoned for a crime I did not commit. I swear I did not murder that man; it was a bandit who killed him, and then fled into the hills as I approached. But I was examining the man for signs of life when the authorities rode up. They arrested me and threw me in prison without even a trial.

" 'My only friend in prison was an old man, so peculiar in his behavior that the guards thought he was mad. I found him to be kindly enough, perhaps erratic in his thoughts, but brilliant in many ways.

" 'Soon after we became friends he mentioned his treasure. I had no idea what he meant, but did not pry into his secrets. Later he told me that he had spent most of his adult life searching the mountain valleys for Mexican opals, which are quite valuable in the world gem market. In one remote valley, at the foot of a small waterfall, he had found an incredibly rich deposit of opals, which he had carried out in a small leather bag.

" 'The local bandit chief, who was also the sheriff and judge, learned of my friend's find. The old man was arrested, but not before he had safely hidden the leather bag.

" 'The old man was thrown into prison on a false charge, just as I was. He told me that if I would help him escape he would lead me to the opals, and divide them with me.

" 'My love, I shan't attempt to tell you how I managed our escape, for I am weakening. But I *did* lead the old man from the prison by the faint light of a new moon. Somehow we managed to walk many miles before dawn. Once we were away from the prison, the old man led the way.

" 'At last we came to a shed on an abandoned farm. The old man used a flat rock to dig into the ground inside the shed. He pulled forth a leather bag, and spilled out the contents into his lap. Such a sight in the light of dawn! Scores of gleaming gems!

" 'Although I protested that the stones were his, he was as good as his word. He divided the opals into two piles, placed one pile in the leather bag, and handed it to me. We stood up. He put his frail arms around me, gave me a hug, and walked away. I never saw him again.

" 'I was able to sell a few of my gems outside Juarez, and bought a horse and some supplies. At last I had the grubstake we had so long dreamed about, and more. If only I could reach you safely with it.

" 'That whole territory from Mexico up through Texas and then through the border states is very dangerous, my love. There has been a breakdown of law and order. All men of authority have been in one army or another, leaving only the undesirables to rule locally by force of arms. I have had many narrow escapes from bandits and bushwhackers while trying to reach you.

" 'And I have come so close to reaching you! But now I know it is not to be.

" 'I am writing this final letter to you, my love, as a means of conveying to you, at long last, our grubstake. And somehow I must do it secretly, for I'm sure this letter will be read by others. I have devised such a way. Only you will know my meaning.

" 'I am in a cave *twenty yards from a point where three streams come together, near Riverton.* I have hidden, in this vicinity, the leather pouch containing the opals. Here are my clues to the hiding place.

" 'Somewhere in the clock, I fashioned a secret compartment. Inside that compartment is my will, leaving everything I own to you. There is a name mentioned in my will. Let this be the riddle you must solve.

" '*The name is upside down. Beneath it you will find the opals—the final gift I can bestow on you.*' "

≈ 8 ≈

Death in a Cave

"The name is upside down. Beneath it you will find the opals." Daphne repeated the riddle in a whisper.

"What does that mean?" Shoie walked over and stared at the clock.

"I don't know," said Christina. "I've been puzzling over it since the first time I read the letter. In fact, it was the letter that brought me here to Riverton. I was trying to get over the death of my husband. Tim's letter mentioned that the cave where he lay dying was near the town of Riverton, Indiana. I came here on the slim chance that I could find the cave. Actually, I was looking for anything to do to keep my mind off Jim's death. I arrived ten days ago, and found this lovely little home for rent, furnished as you see it except for Jim's photograph and the clock. I have rented it for three months while the owner is on an extended trip."

Alvin's thoughts were elsewhere. He was tugging at the lobe of his left ear, which was a sure sign that the Magnificent Brain was in full operation.

"The clock is ticking now," he said. He scratched the back of his neck, where the makeup was beginning to itch. "How come?"

"I tried my best to find a secret compartment in the clock. Thanks to Tim's fine craftsmanship, there was no clue to its existence, as far as I was concerned. My cousin said she had looked too, but finally figured Tim must have been talking about another clock, and she lost interest in the whole mystery. The day after I arrived I took the clock to Mr. Briggs, who was recommended to me, and asked him to see if he could repair it. Because I didn't know him personally, I didn't mention the possibility of a secret compartment."

"I know him," said the Pest. She knew everyone in Riverton. "The watch and clock man. He's nice."

"He was fascinated with the old clock. He said he thought he could put it back in running order, but it would take a few days. There was no way he could get replacements for the worn parts, so he'd have to hand-make them himself. I could tell he looked on it as a challenge."

Alvin scratched his forehead. One of the age lines came off on his fingers. It made his face a bit lopsided.

"Yesterday Mr. Briggs called," Christina continued, "and said the clock was back in fine working order. He also said he had discovered something special about the clock.

"I hurried right over to his shop. When I walked in he was waiting on two customers. One man's face was covered

with a black beard. The other was a heavyset man with a lopsided nose."

"The men outside, just a few minutes ago!" exploded Shoie. "The men who tried to steal your purse!"

"Yes. The bearded man told Mr. Briggs to go ahead and wait on me. I had a bad feeling about those two men. It flashed through my mind that they might be waiting for an opportunity to steal some jewelry from Mr. Briggs. When he went to the back room for the clock, I kept my eye on them.

"A minute later he returned, and carefully placed the clock on the countertop. 'Here it is,' he said proudly, 'as good as new. And I have a surprise for you. I so much admired the artistry in this clock that I checked every piece of wood. And guess what I found. Look right along here.'

"He pointed to the heavy base of the clock. There was the faintest of lines there, as though the wood had barely started to split. He took a pin and pried at the line. A large part of the board popped loose, revealing the secret compartment. And in the compartment was this envelope. It was labeled LAST WILL OF TIMOTHY MARTIN.

"When I saw the writing, I exclaimed without realizing what I was saying, 'The key to the treasure! The will tells where the opals are hidden!'

"I suddenly realized that the two strangers were very interested in what I was saying. They had stepped closer so they could examine the secret compartment themselves. I quickly folded the envelope and put it in my purse. The bearded man was watching me intently.

" 'Thank you very much, Mr. Briggs,' I said. 'I'll come back tomorrow and settle my bill.' I carried out the clock, and hurried home to read the will."

"Those two guys know there's a treasure hidden some-where," said Alvin. "And they know that the will is the key to it. That's why they were trying to snatch your purse."

The Pest shivered. "I don't like their looks. Alvin, Beardface glared at you like he'd get you if it was the last thing he ever did." She shivered again.

"There's not a thing to worry about," said Alvin. "They don't even know I exist."

"What do you mean, old man?" asked Shoie.

"That's exactly what I am in their eyes. An old man. My disguise was perfect, and if the bearded man sees me on the street without the disguise, he won't have any idea that I was the little old man."

"That's true," admitted the Pest.

Alvin moved to the center of the room. His face still had many of the wrinkles of an old man, but his voice was vibrant. "Now, let's analyze this situation step-by-step," he said crisply.

"The Magnificent Brain flashes into action," said Shoie.

Alvin tried to suppress his excitement. "Get the will, and let's see what name is mentioned in it. Then we'll solve the riddle and find the opals."

"Sorry, Alvin, but we can't see the will until tomorrow. After I read it, I rented a safety deposit box at the bank, and put it inside."

"Okay. We'll take a look tomorrow."

"It's so sad that Tim died all alone," said the Pest. "In that awful cave. He didn't get to see Ada ever again. After he found their grubstake."

There was silence in the room.

≈ 9 ≈

The Riddle

At nine-thirty the following morning Christina returned from the bank to find the kids waiting on her
front porch.

Christina sat down on a rocking chair. Alvin and Shoie
were vigorously swinging in the porch swing, and the Pest
was seated on the top step, her slim little back leaning
against the rail.

"Did you get Tim's will?" asked Alvin. The squeak of the
porch swing stopped abruptly.

Christina nodded. She removed an envelope from her
purse, and from the envelope she took a brittle piece of
paper.

"We're about to solve Tim's riddle," said Alvin con-
fidently.

"Solve Tim's riddle," repeated Daphne.

"Just crank the will through the Magnificent Brain and out comes the solution," declared Shoie.

"I'm afraid it's not going to be that easy," said Christina. "I read the will again while I was at the bank. I can't see that there's any solution to the riddle."

She unfolded the piece of paper carefully. "Here's what the will says: 'I am about to embark upon a journey that may be dangerous. I therefore leave this behind as my last will and testament. I hereby leave all my worldly goods to my beloved betrothed, Ada Scheuneman, with the following exceptions: To my good friend Tyler Jackson I leave all the tools of my trade in the hope that he will find them helpful in establishing his own cabinetmaking business; and to my younger brother Hebron Martin I leave my horse Ginger if that horse still be alive at the time this will becomes effective as a result of the death of the undersigned. Signed Timothy Martin. Witnessed Benjamin Hardin.' "

Shoie broke the silence. "There are only two names in the will."

Alvin had a glazed look, as though a curtain had fallen across his eyes. "There are three names," he corrected.

"Two," insisted Shoie. "There are only two names. He left his tools to somebody named Tyler Jackson and his horse to his younger brother Hebron."

Alvin tugged at his right ear. "There was another name in the will. The first name mentioned was that of Ada Scheuneman, the woman he planned to marry."

The motion of the swing stopped. "That's right, old bean. Now we have three names to puzzle over."

"You're both wrong," piped up Daphne. "There are four names in the will. How about the man who signed it as a witness? What was his name again?"

Christina looked at the sheet of paper. "Benjamin Hardin. And there's still another name. Tim Martin's own name."

The swing started squeaking again.

"Tim Martin and Ada Scheuneman," recited Alvin. "Tyler Jackson and Hebron Martin. And Benjamin Hardin." The Magnificent Brain nibbled around the edges of the riddle. "What do we know about them that might help solve the puzzle?"

"We know quite a lot about Ada Scheuneman," said Christina. "I have a rather complete record of her life. Her birth, marriage, children, and her death are all entered in the old family Bible. She apparently never tried to look for the treasure. With Tim gone, and married to Thor now, she didn't want to reopen that chapter in her life."

"I don't see how *her* name in the will has anything to do with the location of the treasure," said the Pest.

"I agree," said Shoie.

"Do you know anything about Tyler Jackson?" Alvin asked.

"Practically nothing. He was younger than Tim. Kind of an apprentice, learning Tim's trade. Tim mentions him in one or two of his early letters. That's about all I know about him."

"How about Hebron?"

"Hebron's name appears in the Bible and in other records. He died of tuberculosis when he was twenty-four years old. Several times Tim mentioned Hebron in his letters. It's obvious he was very fond of his younger brother. That's about all I can tell you."

"And Benjamin Hardin?"

"I know absolutely nothing about him. My guess is that he was a neighbor whom Tim called in to witness the will. I've never seen his name anywhere else."

The swing moved faster. "We seem to be working our way up a blind alley," said Alvin. "There's no obvious clue to the puzzle in any one of the names. Yet Tim was certain that Ada could solve the mystery."

"You know what I think?" declared the Pest. She didn't wait for an answer. "I think Tim knew something about one of those persons that we don't know, and never will know. I think he knew something special. And I don't think we'll ever find out what it is."

"I think you're right, dear," said Christina softly.

Alvin closed his eyes and recited the words that he knew by heart: " 'The name is upside down. Beneath it you will find the opals'. Tim Martin. Hebron Martin. Ada Scheuneman. Tyler Jackson. Benjamin Hardin."

Alvin tugged harder at his ear. The porch swing groaned.

≈10≈

A Girl Scout
Sells Cookies

Alvin Fernald stared at his reflection in the mirror and couldn't believe what he saw.

"Perfect!" exclaimed the Pest with a giggle.

Shoie fell to the floor and pretended to beat the floorboards.

The kids were again in the costume room of the Summer Theater. They were back at what had become their favorite sport—disguising Alvin for the day. This morning they had found a Girl Scout uniform from some long-forgotten play.

Now Alvin gazed critically at his image in the floor-length mirror. Gazing back at him was a rather pretty, slim Girl Scout with long blond hair. Alvin turned his head, and the hair rippled across his shoulders. There was just a hint of pale lipstick on his lips, and his cheeks were brightened with just the slightest touch of rouge. The Girl Scout hat perched saucily atop his head.

"What's your name, old bean?" gasped Shoie, still pounding the floor.

Alvin considered the question quite seriously. "Adele Claphorn," he said at last in a high little voice. "My name is Adele Claphorn, and I belong to Troop twenty-one of the Riverton Girl Scouts. You wanna buy some cookies?"

"Buy some cookies?" repeated Daphne with a giggle.

Still looking in the mirror, Alvin batted his eyelashes at Shoie. "How about being my boyfriend in school this year, big guy?"

"Not on your life." Shoie leaped to his feet in dismay.

"Alvin, what are we going to do today, now that we have you in disguise?"

"We're just going to fool around. Come on. Let's go downtown and have some fun."

As they approached Finney's Drugstore, Shoie and Daphne dropped back so they wouldn't be seen with Adele.

Mr. Finney was just coming out the door with a broom in his hand. He looked up. Alvin skipped toward him. Mr. Finney looked him straight in the eye. He had known Alvin for many years. Now there was not a hint of recognition.

"Good morning," said Mr. Finney with a nod.

"Hi," said Alvin in a squeaky voice. He was thinking of the time, years ago, when he had motorized the Pest's tricycle. She had wheeled crazily along Main Street, zigging and zagging, with pedestrians leaping for their lives. At the last moment the tricycle had veered into Mr. Finney's drugstore and struck a towering display of the Special of the Week, Hi-Soak Disposable Diapers. The display had exploded. One diaper had even landed on the fan circling slowly overhead.

"Hi, Mr. Finney," Alvin said in his piping voice.

Mr. Finney smiled. "Do I know you, little lady?"

"My name is Adele Claphorn. I live over on Oak Street."

"Oh. Well, you *do* look familiar. Don't tell me it's time to buy Girl Scout cookies already."

"Oh, no. The reason I'm wearing my uniform is that my troop is having a picnic down at Weasel River Park today."

"Well, have fun. And you can bring me a box of cookies when you're out selling them." He turned to go back into his store.

"I'll do that," said Alvin in his own deep voice.

Mr. Finney tossed a startled look over his shoulder. "Did you say that?"

"Say what?" asked Alvin in Adele's high voice.

"About doing that. Bringing cookies."

"Oh. Yes."

"Your voice sounded different."

"Frog in my throat. Gotta go now. Bye-bye." Alvin waved daintily and skipped down the street.

At the police station, Alvin asked for his father. He was told that Sergeant Fernald was out on a call. While he was in the station Alvin took early orders for thirteen boxes of Girl Scout cookies from policemen whom he had known most of his life. Officer Maynard remarked, "Girlie, with that long blond hair you're some cute cooky yourself. I'll bet Sergeant Fernald's kid would really go for you. We'll have to try to match you up."

Alvin turned away in consternation just as Shoie and

Daphne came through the revolving door. He pretended not to see them, but as he passed he whispered, "Meet me outside by the fountain. Hurry!"

Alvin-Adele sat on the low wall that encircled the fountain in front of city hall. The other kids quickly joined him. There was an expression of tension on the Girl Scout's face.

"What's up, old bean?" asked Shoie. "Why the big hurry to meet out here?"

Alvin glanced quickly around. There was no one within earshot. "I have to go to the bathroom," he whispered urgently.

"So what's wrong with that? Go on back into city hall."

"But which one shall I go to?" Alvin spit out the words. "I can't go to either one dressed like this."

An understanding look flashed across Shoie's face. The Pest started grinning.

"OHHHHHHHH!" they said in unison.

≈ 11 ≈

A Conversation
with Beardface

An hour later, Alvin was still disguised as a Girl Scout
but was tired of playing the part. The kids walked
down Mulberry Street, out on the edge of town, heading
back toward the Summer Theater. Alvin scratched above
his ear. The wig made his head itch like fury.

Houses were far apart out here. Empty lots were overgrown with weeds.

"Look!" said the Pest. She stopped walking.

"What's the matter?" Alvin stopped too.

"There's someone living in old Mrs. Brinkley's house. At
least there's a car in the driveway behind the fence."

Old Mrs. Brinkley had died a year before. Her house,
still furnished, had stood empty until now. It was a big old
house built of gray stone. There was a long porch across the
front, still filled with rocking chairs and a porch swing that
had been there when the old widow had died. Now the

lawn in front of the house was overgrown with weeds. Around the house ran a high iron picket fence. The pickets were held together by crossbars top and bottom. And each picket ended in a pointed spike that extended several inches above the top crossbar. Mrs. Brinkley had installed the fence to keep out the burglars she believed were constantly after her money.

The big iron gate was closed across the driveway, but through the bars of the gate Alvin could see a car.

"I wonder who's living there," said Shoie.

"We'll ask Daddy," said Daphne. "He knows everything that goes on in Riverton."

"Let's take a closer look," said Alvin.

The kids walked slowly up the sidewalk toward the house. Suddenly Alvin stopped. "I thought so," he said.

"You thought *what* so?" asked Shoie.

"Take a look at the car. See anything familiar, old man?"

Shoie peered intently through the fence at the car. "Well, it's a tan car, almost copper-colored. Looks like a four-door sedan. Maybe a Pontiac. And it has an Illinois license."

"Do you realize what you have just described?"

Daphne gasped. "The bad guys' car! The ones who are after Christina's treasure!"

"Sure looks like it," said Shoie.

"Well, there's one way to find out," said Alvin. "You guys stay out of sight."

"What are you going to do, Alvin?" Daphne was worried.

"I'm going to sell them some cookies. At least I'm going to try."

"Oh, Alvin! Don't do it! They're mean. Maybe they'll hurt you."

"They won't even recognize me," said Alvin. "It's me, Alvin Fernald, Master of a Thousand Disguises."

Shoie and Daphne hid behind a huge maple tree.

Alvin sauntered up the sidewalk. Occasionally he had visited Mrs. Brinkley before she died. Once she had paid him to rake her lawn. Alvin therefore knew the layout of the house and yard.

There was a button beside the big iron gate. He took a deep breath, adjusted his skirt, and pushed it.

Nothing happened.

He pushed again, holding his finger on the button for at least thirty seconds.

Finally the front door opened. A prickle of excitement ran up Alvin's back as he saw a bearded head emerge.

"Go away, little girl!" the man shouted. He slammed the door.

It made Alvin even more determined to talk to the man. He pressed the button again.

The front door swung open so hard it slammed against the side of the house. The bearded man filled the doorway. "I said go away!"

"Uckelty muck," said Alvin softly. He didn't want the man to hear clearly; he wanted Beardface to come closer so he could make a positive identification.

"What? What did you say?"

"Uckelty muck. Mini mush Daphne. Igglety poof Shoie. Uckelty muck."

The gibberish worked. The man crossed the porch in

three strides and came bounding down the steps. He stopped on the other side of the fence and glared at Alvin. "I told you to get out of here, girlie. Now get! Whatever you're selling I don't want."

Sweat was trickling down Alvin's back. "Girl Scout cookies," he said in a high, quiet voice. "Do you want to buy some Girl Scout cookies? I'll deliver them right here to your door sometime next month."

The bearded man gazed bleakly at him. Suddenly he said, "Haven't I seen you somewhere before?"

Alvin tossed his curls. He gave Beardface his most fetching smile. "I don't believe so, mister. Anyway, will you buy some cookies?"

"No. No cookies. No more talk. Nothing else. And if I ever see you again, you'll be very, very sorry."

"Okay. Sure. Okay. No harm done. I was only asking."

≈12≈

Intruders in the House

After their encounter with Beardface, the kids returned to the Summer Theater. Alvin shed his Girl Scout uniform.

The kids had lunch, and then Alvin phoned Christina. He intended to tell her about the two bad guys living in old Mrs. Brinkley's house. But Christina asked if the kids could meet her at the library right away. She wanted to examine some county maps to see whether she could spot any possible places where Tim had hidden in the cave. "You children know the area around Riverton better than anyone I know. Maybe we can locate a place where three streams come together. Will you help?"

At the library, Alvin told Christina about his encounter with Beardface that morning. "He and Broken Nose have probably rented Mrs. Brinkley's house while they try to get their hands on the treasure," he said.

The news upset Christina. She had hoped, after the fight in front of her house, that the men had left town.

"Let's get busy," said Alvin resolutely. "Forget those guys. Let's find Tim's cave."

They spent almost two hours studying maps of the county. They even examined maps more than a hundred years old, just in case some of the streams had dried up. But they failed to find any point where three streams came together.

At last Christina was ready to give up. "Let's go back to my house and study every word of Tim's letter again. Maybe we'll find another clue."

When Christina unlocked her front door and pushed it open, she gasped, then burst into tears. Alvin pushed his way past her.

Never had he seen such a mess. The sofa was over-turned. Cushions had been hurled this way and that. Drapes were strewn across the floor. Drawers had been dumped everywhere. In the kitchen, most of the dishes, pots, and pans had been pulled out of the cabinets. In Christina's bedroom the mattress had been slashed and the filling ripped out.

Alvin checked the back door. The lock had been pried open with a crowbar.

Christina sat down on one of her kitchen chairs. Tears rolled down her cheeks. Daphne walked over and put her arms around her.

Alvin cleared his throat. "Crying won't do any good. We'll all pitch in and clear up this mess. But first let's figure out what happened and why."

"What happened and why," echoed the Pest.

"I think we all know who did it. Beardface and Broken Nose. They must have been planning it when I talked to Beardface this morning."

Shoie turned to Christina. "How did they know you'd be gone long enough to search your house?"

Christina dabbed at her tears, then sat up straight. "I can tell you that. Right after I talked with you on the phone, Alvin, someone called and said he was a distant cousin from New Hampshire, in town for a few days. Wanted to see me. I told him I'd be gone for a couple of hours, but that I'd make it a point to be home all morning tomorrow. He said he'd stop by then."

"That explains how he knew you'd be gone. And I think we all know why they were here. They were looking for Tim's letter. Did you leave it here, Christina?"

"Yes. It and the will. Oh, my goodness!" Christina jumped to her feet and ran to the living room. Instantly she put her hand to her lips. "They're gone!"

"How do you know?" asked Alvin.

"Where were they hidden?" asked Shoie.

"I'll bet I know!" exclaimed Alvin. "You hid them in the secret compartment in the clock—the same hiding place Tim used more than a hundred years ago." He gazed up at the clock on the mantel. The compartment was open; there was nothing inside.

"No," said Christina. "They learned of the secret compartment in the clock shop, so I hid the letter and the will somewhere else." There was a note of anguish in her voice.

Alvin glanced at her. She was looking at the portrait of

her husband Jim. The frame had been smashed across the edge of the table. The photograph itself was crumpled and torn.

"I hid Tim's will and his letter behind Jim's picture, inside the frame. And now look what I've done." She picked up the tattered photo.

"You didn't do anything," said Daphne. "But those terrible men did."

≈13≈

Master Plan X

Alvin sat on his bed, with Shoie beside him. Daphne, practicing her yoga, had assumed the lotus position on the floor at their feet.

The previous afternoon it had taken them four hours to help Christina clean up the mess at her house.

"We've got to strike back at those horrible, horrible men," said Daphne. There was a hard edge of bitterness in her voice. "But what can we do?"

"We can get Tim's letter back," said Alvin. "And his will, too."

"You're out of your skull," said Shoie in a quiet voice. "Those two guys would make mincemeat of us."

"I have a plan," said Alvin, tugging at his right earlobe.

"Have a plan," said the Pest, putting one slim ankle behind her neck.

"We need information," said Alvin in a distant voice.

"We need to overhear them talking between themselves. We need to know their plans. Sooner or later they'll mention the location of Tim's will."

"You planning to slip down the chimney like Santa Claus, old bean?"

"No. A better disguise than that. There are more than fifty disguises at the Summer Theater. But the Magnificent Brain has come up with the simplest, most masterful disguise of all."

"Disguise? What kind of disguise?"

"Something that blends completely into the background. Something that no one would consider to be a human being."

"Something, something," said the Pest. "What kind of something?"

"A rock."

"A *rock?*" Daphne and Shoie said it in unison.

"A rock. A rock never looks suspicious. It's just *there*. People never pay any attention to a rock." He paused. "Perfect. I'll disguise myself as a rock and get all the information we need."

"You've flipped, old bean. You're absolutely bonkers. The Magnificent Brain has overzapped itself, burned out all its circuits. How are you going to disguise yourself as a rock?"

"Gunnysacks. Basement. Spray paint." The words tumbled out. Alvin leaped to his feet and headed for the door.

He went straight to an old cabinet in one corner of the basement. From the bottom shelf he pulled half a dozen old gunnysacks. He unfolded one sack and held it up. It was a very large sack that once had held potatoes. Alvin gave the bag a snap, and dust floated through the basement. He carried the sack into his father's workshop, where he studied the labels on a row of spray-paint cans.

"Ah. Yes. Just what we want."

The label read BATTLESHIP GRAY. FAST DRYING.

Alvin handed the gunnysack to Shoie. "Hold it up."

Shoie held out the sack. He did a little dance like a bullfighter waving his cape. Alvin shook the can, then began spraying the sack in long sweeping strokes. The sack turned gray.

"Other side," said Alvin.

Shoie turned the sack around, and Alvin resumed spraying. He looked over at the Pest, swinging his arm, forgetting that his finger was still on the spray button. "This time you won't even have to apply any makeup. I'll just—"

"GLOBBLEGOOF! MUGGLE!"

Alvin snapped his head around. The hissing paint sprayed Shoie's face. In an instant, that face turned battleship gray. Alvin stopped the spray.

Shoie opened his eyes. "Does this paint wash off with soap and water?" he asked, two white eyes gleaming from the gray mask.

Alvin read the label. He forced out a reply. "No. Clean up with turpentine."

An hour later they gave up on Shoie's face. It was a mottled blotch of gray and red—gray from the paint and red from trying to rub it off with turpentine.

"You don't smell very good, Shoie," said Daphne in a sweet voice.

Shoie cradled her neck in his elbow as though to throttle her. Actually he was very fond of the Pest.

"Well, at least the paint on the gunnysack is dry," said Alvin. "Come on. We have work to do if we're going to be ready by tonight."

"Tonight, old bean?"

"Tonight. We strike at dusk. Master Plan X."

Darkness was falling as the three kids made their way along alleys and through backyards so they wouldn't be spotted. They made a strange sight. Alvin was dressed in the gunnysack, which fell below his knees. His arms and head were completely enclosed. He had cut a small hole in the front so he could peek out, but the hole kept moving away from his eyes. The sack was still filled with dust, and he kept sneezing.

Shoie had a hand on one of Alvin's shoulders, and pushed him this way and that. Alvin had trouble climbing the Tuttles' fence, and he dropped into their yard with a thud. Then, after he had regained his footing, he stumbled into Mrs. Tuttle's wire clothesline, and found himself on the ground once again, rubbing his Adam's apple.

"We're almost there," whispered Shoie.

"Don't forget Master Plan X." Alvin's voice was muffled as he struggled to his feet. "You've got to lure them away from the gate so I can slip through."

"Righto, old bean."

Shoie guided Alvin along the fence that guarded old Mrs. Brinkley's house. At last they stood silently in front of the gate. Alvin readjusted the hole so he could see. He looked toward the house. There was one dim light inside.

"Are you sure you know exactly what you are going to do, Daphne?" Only in times of emergency did he call his sister by her real name; it was a sure sign that Alvin was worried.

"I'll be all right. Don't worry."

Suddenly a voice shouted. "Who's that? Who's out there?"

Alvin almost panicked. "They're on the porch!" he whispered. "They're sitting in the darkness on the porch!"

"That's just what we want," whispered Shoie urgently. "We want them to come out here."

"Right. Okay, you guys. Execute Master Plan X."

Alvin moved over to one side of the gate. He dropped to his knees and huddled up against the iron fence. His face was totally hidden inside the folds of the gray gunnysack. Alvin Fernald, Master of a Thousand Disguises, was an indistinguishable blob.

Shoie rang the bell. He kept punching the button at short intervals.

The Pest's voice shrilled through the darkness, chanting words she had made up especially for the occasion:

"Come out, you nasty men, come out—
Come out the gate, we'll make you shout,
You'll run and dance, oh fiddle-dee-dee,
You'll jump around just like a flea."

Alvin groaned. *What a terrible poet!*

There were curses from the porch, then the sound of feet coming down the wooden steps. Shoie stood his ground. The Pest leaned her trembling body against him.

In the semidarkness the kids could make out Beardface as he approached the gate. Just behind lumbered Broken Nose, his breath coming in short gasps.

Beardface spoke in a voice so soft it was especially threatening. "Leave. Right now. For good. We know who you kids are—and that you're involved with Christina Moller."

Shoie had rehearsed what he had to say, but it took all his courage to say it. "And *we* know what you stole from behind her husband's picture."

There was a sudden intake of breath on the other side of the gate.

"And we know where you've hidden it," added Shoie.

Alvin's heart was racing so fast that he knew the sack must be trembling. He had told Shoie to say that they knew the hiding place. It was a bluff, but it might lead to valuable information.

"And we're on our way to tell the police right now!" exclaimed Daphne. "Come out, you nasty men, and see— you'll jump around just like a flea!"

The gate rattled as the bearded man unlocked it from inside, and jerked it open. The two men confronted the two kids—with a large gray stone at their feet.

"You're not going to tell anyone," said Beardface in his soft threatening voice. "We're going to take you two kids inside the house and find out everything you know."

Beardface jumped toward Daphne, and Broken Nose reached out to grab Shoie.

Daphne ran up the street toward the Tuttles' house. Shoie ran in the opposite direction.

Daphne could hear the man's footsteps pounding along behind her. Suddenly she veered into the Tuttles' side yard. The man was so close she was sure to be caught. She made a final, desperate lunge beneath Mrs. Tuttle's nearly invisible clothesline. An instant later there was a strangled "ARRRRRGH!" and the sound of a body falling to the ground.

Daphne ducked around the Tuttles' garage and shot up the trunk of the apple tree in the back yard. It was one of her favorite climbing trees in town. Even in the dark, each limb was a familiar step, and she shot up between the branches. Huddled in the top, she looked down. The dim figure of Beardface staggered into view. He looked slowly around, then turned and walked back the way he had come, rubbing his throat.

Meanwhile, Broken Nose was no match for the Greatest Athlete in Roosevelt School. Shoie played with the heavyset man. He led him up Myrtle Street, then suddenly veered and vaulted over Willy Manfred's fence. He stood on the other side as the man laboriously climbed the fence rails and dropped to the ground.

Shoie darted off again. He ran up the hill in front of Mike Shuck's place. It was the best hill in town for sledding because it was so steep. When he saw that the man was losing ground, he slowed to a walk. The man came puffing up the hill. Under the streetlight at the top, he stopped.

His hands fell to his knees, and he gasped in exhaustion.

Shoie darted over and touched Broken Nose on the shoulder. The man lunged at him, but the extra effort was too much. He toppled to the ground.

The man got painfully to his feet. He glared at Shoie, then without a word he staggered back down Shuck's hill, legs wobbling.

So far, thought Shoie, *Master Plan X is working to perfection.*

Five minutes later Daphne joined Shoie in the bushes across the street from Mrs. Brinkley's house. Shoie touched his finger to his lips, then motioned her to follow him.

He sneaked along the street, then darted across through a patch of darkness. They made their way silently along the iron fence until they stood at the gate.

Low, angry voices came from the porch.

And in the dim light coming through the front window, they could make out a large gray stone lying in the bushes close to the porch.

It was a stone that had not been there before.

≈ 14 ≈

Inside the Stone

Alvin could see nothing, but heard everything.
Footsteps scuffed along the sidewalk. TROMP TROMP TROMP up the wooden steps. There were short gasps as one man tried to regain his breath. The creak of the porch floorboards. Then the squeak of two rocking chairs, one on each side above Alvin's head.

"I'll kill 'em!" the gasping voice said. "If I ever see those kids again, I'll kill 'em!"

The sound of the other chair rocking. "Yeah. I could throttle that little girl myself. But we'll probably never see them again. We'll likely be leaving in a day or two."

Gasp. "Can't get my breath. Might have had a heart attack. Stupid kid. He runs like a wildcat. Jumps fences like a deer." Gasp. Gasp.

"Well. At least we took care of their friend. We really did a job on that woman's house."

"Yeah. She'll never forget that. I'm glad we had trouble finding those papers. Gave us a chance to really mess up the place."

A grunt of satisfaction.

"She won't rest easy in that torn-up bed."

A cackling laugh that came out as a partial gasp.

The creak of two chairs rocking. On the porch above Alvin's head, Beardface was on his right, Broken Nose on his left.

"Now that we have the papers, we should be able to locate that treasure in short order." It was Beardface's voice.

"What's your plan?"

"I have a strong feeling that the cave is the key to the treasure."

"So? How do we find the cave?"

"We know from the letter that the cave is near Riverton. 'Where three streams flow together.' "

The sound of a car passing by, beyond the fence. Alvin's left leg, twisted under him, was beginning to cramp.

"We can't thrash around the country asking suspicious questions about three creeks." Broken Nose's voice. "We both have records. Let's not alert the police."

"Use your head. We don't just go blundering around. We go to a surveyor's office and ask to see the Coast and Geodetic maps."

"The *what* maps?"

"The Coast and Geodetic maps. They're the most detailed maps in existence. They show every road, every hill, and practically every building. Most important, they show every stream."

Alvin's left leg was in pain. Slowly he moved it to a new position. A twig crackled under him.

"What was that?"

"Yeah. I heard it too. Might be out there in the front yard."

"It could be those kids back again."

"Let's take a look. You go around the house to the right, and I'll go to the left."

"I hope it *is* those kids." There was menace in Broken Nose's voice.

"So do I. More than likely the noise was just a squirrel, or a snake in the bushes."

"Make it the kids, or a squirrel. If there's anything I'm scared of it's snakes."

"Can't say that I like them either."

"Watch your step in the dark."

TROMP TROMP TROMP. Feet came down the steps. Alvin held his breath. Footsteps passed close by his head. He waited until he heard voices calling each other in the back of the house. He wiggled his foot, and repositioned the gunnysack so the little hole was just in front of his eyes. He could see a few square inches of ground in front of his nose.

Footsteps approached. Suddenly the toe of a shoe appeared in front of his eyes.

"I didn't see anything," said Beardface. "Did you?"

"No. Those kids must have made us jittery. Come on."

The shoe disappeared. TROMP TROMP TROMP. Then the squeak of two rocking chairs.

"So we look at these special maps, Harry. How does that help?"

"Don't be stupid. Those maps show every stream in the area. Even the smallest. In blue. Water is always in blue. The only blue on the maps."

"So?"

"So we look at every blue line on the map. And when we find where *three blue lines come together*, that's where we'll find the cave."

"You're pretty sharp, Harry."

"Of course that doesn't mean we'll find the treasure. But I have a hunch the treasure is somewhere around the cave. The guy left a clue to its location. We should be able to find it."

The end of Alvin's nose began to itch.

"What do you suppose the clue means, Harry?"

"I dunno. But we'll find out. First we have to find the cave."

The itch was worse. Alvin felt a sneeze coming on.

"Let's get out the letter and the will and compare them once more," said Beardface. "Maybe we'll come up with something."

"Good idea. Where'd you put them when we came back?"

"I hid them. Nobody would guess where."

"Where?"

"Remember that picture hanging above the fireplace? The picture of the old man?"

"Yeah. Funny looking old geezer."

Alvin risked a sniff.

"Well, I taped the papers to the back of that picture."

"Harry, you're a genius."

"HATCHOOOOOOOOOOOOOOOOO!!!"

"Hey! Who's there?"

"Harry! Harry! That big rock there. I could swear I saw it move!"

TROMPTROMPTROMP.

The rock leaped three feet into the air. Through the hole in the bag Alvin saw the men freeze in surprise. It gave him the two or three seconds he needed to jerk the bag up over his head and fling it at the two men. He fled down the driveway toward the gate.

Heavy footsteps pounded along behind him.

Just as Alvin approached the gate he suddenly realized he would be caught. The gate was locked shut, and he didn't know how to open it.

As he turned to face his pursuers, a voice said urgently, "Over here, Alvin!"

Three steps to the right of the gate, Shoie was poised atop the iron fence. Only the Great Athlete could have made that climb, and then wedged his foot down on the crossbar between the spikes.

Alvin leaped upward, and a hand brushed the heel of his shoe. Shoie grabbed his arm, and he sailed toward the sky. He plopped to the ground, and Shoie landed beside him. The Pest appeared from nowhere.

The three figures fled up the street, paying no attention to the angry shouts behind them.

Only when he was safely perched in the shadowy branches of the Tuttles' apple tree did Alvin feel safe again.

"I found out where Tim's papers are hidden," he said.

"Great show, old bean!" exclaimed Shoie.

Alvin didn't answer. Already, Master Plan Z was taking shape inside the Magnificent Brain.

≈ 15 ≈

The Greatest Disguise in History

"Master Plan Z is born," said Alvin. "In here." He tapped his forehead.

"Cheers!" yelled Shoie, clasping his hands above his head.

"Yeah!" piped up Daphne.

It was the following day. They were in Alvin's room holding another planning session.

"Follow me step-by-step as I reason this out logically," said Alvin. "First we need to recover Tim's letter and his will. It will be Tim's *precise* wording in them that will reveal the location of the treasure. Therefore it's essential that we recover those two documents posthaste."

"Alvin, you always use bigger words when you're explaining something than when you're just talking," observed the Pest.

He pretended she hadn't spoken. "So the first goal of Master Plan Z is to recover the documents."

"And how do you expect to do that, old bean? Just knock on the door, nice as can be, and ask them please to hand over Tim's papers?"

Daphne shivered.

"We'll need help," admitted Alvin. "And luck. But we can do it."

"How?"

"Master Plan Z will make use of a mammoth disguise. Quite literally the greatest disguise in history."

"Ho, ho! Now he's making history."

"No. Just *using* history. This disguise was used thousands of years ago. It became the most famous disguise of all time. And it probably was the biggest disguise ever known. I've been thinking a lot about it, and I'm sure we can make that same disguise work for us."

"Don't keep us in suspense, Alvin," said the Pest. "Tell us what you mean."

"We learned about it when we were studying ancient history last year. Do you remember, Shoie?"

"I don't have the foggiest idea what you're talking about, Alvin."

"Pest, run downstairs and get that one-volume encyclopedia out of the bookcase."

Daphne skipped out of the room and returned a minute later with a very large book. Alvin took it from her, placed it on the bed, and thumbed through the pages. He stopped and put his finger on a place in the book. He nodded in satisfaction.

"Our problem," he said, looking up, "is that there is a high fence around old Mrs. Brinkley's place. We must get several people inside. The only way is through the gate. But the gate is always locked."

"We know all that," complained Shoie. "Just tell us Master Plan Z."

"The Greeks, a zillion years ago, had the same problem when they tried to capture the city of Troy. Here's what the encyclopedia says: 'The Greeks besieged Troy for ten years. In all that time, they could not fight their way through the gate. At last they resorted to deceit and disguise. They pretended to abandon their camp, but left behind, in front of the gate, a large wooden horse. Several warriors were hidden inside. At last the Trojans' curiosity won over, and they opened the gates and dragged the huge horse inside the walls. That night, after the city was quiet, the Greek warriors crept from their hiding place inside the horse and opened the gates to their companions, who had quietly returned. The battle was soon over thanks to the wooden horse that carried a handful of warriors through the gates.' "

"Wow! Some disguise, old man!"

"Could we, Alvin?" The Pest was instantly interested. "I mean, could we build a wooden horse and get through the gate?"

"If the Greeks did it, I don't see why we can't. We'll build our own Trojan horse. We're going to need lots of help. We need Kelvy Brown, first of all. He's a good carpenter. And we'll need several other kids. Some inside the horse, and some waiting outside the gate."

"Oh, Alvin, I'm so excited!"

"Shoie, you go find Kelvy and send him right over here. Then line up six or eight kids from Roosevelt School who are willing to help us out today, and then again tonight. Be sure to include Peanuts Dunkle. Have two or three of the kids help you pick up a couple of those old packing crates that were thrown out behind the foundry. Bring them here to our garage. We'll need them for lumber. Have the rest of the kids show up right away at the Summer Theater. Pest, you run over there and get out the scariest costumes you can find. Really horrible stuff.

"Okay, gang. Move!"

≈16≈

An Army at the Gates

K elvy Brown rubbed the palm of his hand over the tip
of his nose in a circular motion. He always rubbed
his nose when he was studying his own craftsmanship. He
put down his hammer. "What do you think, Alvin?"

The late afternoon sun slanted through the maple leaves,
casting shimmery shadows on the driveway.

Alvin took a step backward and studied the work of the
afternoon.

They had started by lashing together four coaster wagons borrowed from garages throughout the neighborhood.
Upon this mobile base they had placed one of the big
packing boxes, but only after Kelvy had altered the box in
several secret and masterful ways according to Alvin's instructions. One alteration was a secret compartment in the
bottom of the box. Working from a crude sketch Alvin had

provided, Kelvy had sawed up the lumber from the second box and used it to fashion a long neck that ended in something that looked vaguely like a horse's head.

"Looks goofy," said Alvin critically.

"Well, I did the best I could," said Kelvy defensively. "Besides, you didn't make a very good drawing."

"Whoa, Kelvy. Calm down. You didn't let me finish. It looks goofy, and that's just what we want. *Exactly* what we want. The goofier the better. We want it so goofy those bad guys will get curious about what it is and why it's there. *Real* curious. So curious they can't resist finding out all about it."

Shoie came walking up the alley munching an apple. He stopped suddenly. "Hey! That thing looks goofy. Looks more like a charging bull than a horse. The ears are so long they look like horns. And who ever heard of a *square neck?*"

Kelvy picked up the hammer and handed it to Shoie. "Here. Let's see you build a round one."

"Aw, c'mon Kelvy, I was only kidding."

"Did you get the other kids, Shoie?" broke in Alvin.

"Yep. Worm's ready to go, along with Spider Funsterman and Tex Crawford."

"What about Peanuts Dunkle?"

"Yeah, him too. And Seth Snyder, except that Seth insists on bringing along his little brother Joey and his littlest brother Runt."

A calculating look spread across Alvin's face. Seth and his two brothers were the only kids in town who could build a "three-high." Runt would climb atop Joey's shoulders, and then Seth would put both brothers atop his own shoulders to form a towering "three-high" that staggered this way and that.

"Great!" said Alvin, rubbing his hands. "They'll fit right into my plans. Where are all the kids now?"

"They're over at the Summer Theater. I told them all about Master Plan Z. They think it's great. Right now the Pest is lining up a costume for each of them. Tonight at six-thirty they'll return to the Summer Theater, and the Pest will apply any makeup they need. Then they meet us at seven-thirty at Weasel Park, in costume, rarin' to go."

"So am I," said Alvin. "Rarin' to go."

Shoie and Kelvy, both large and strong for their age, were selected to pull the Trojan horse. Alvin and Daphne walked along behind. They chose an obscure route up side streets and down alleys. But still they were seen in the light of the half-moon.

"Hey, Alvin, what's that thing?" shouted Ardelle Craigmiller from her backyard. When Alvin didn't answer, she fell into step beside him.

"You guys practicing for a bullfight?" asked Otto Harmon. He, too, joined the parade.

The Trojan horse rumbled into Weasel River Park.

A cheer went up. Eight other kids had gathered there. They sat on top of a picnic table. Each held a sack containing a costume.

Alvin climbed onto a nearby bench so everyone could see him.

"This isn't all fun and games," he began in a low voice. The kids grew quiet. "It could well be dangerous. If any of you want to back out, go ahead." No one moved.

"Good. It's only three blocks over to old Mrs. Brinkley's house. We'll pull the Trojan horse over to the vacant lot just this side of it. There are some alder bushes along the far side of the lot. We'll stop there. The rest of you follow along just as quietly as you can. Shoie has already told you what we'll try to do, once the Trojan horse is in place. Any questions?"

"Who gets to ride in the horse?" asked Peanuts.

"Kelvy, Tex Crawford, Daphne, and myself." Alvin had chosen the insiders long before they had even finished the horse. Kelvy had earned a place in the horse with his carpentry; Tex was small and agile; and Alvin wanted to keep his little sister close by his side.

"Any other questions?" Silence. "Okay, gang. Get into your costumes and let's go. If anyone asks any questions along the way, just say that we're going to an early Halloween party. Which I guess we are, in a funny kind of way."

The Trojan horse groaned to a halt in the clump of alders. The rest of the kids sneaked up to form a circle around it. There was very little light, but Alvin laughed aloud when he saw the costumes. Perfect!

Kelvy ran his hand along the side of the horse until he felt a wooden block. He pressed it. As if by magic, one side of the horse swung away on hinges that Kelvy had concealed inside.

Kelvy lifted out a false floor. Alvin placed the coil of rope he was carrying inside the compartment, and Kelvy tossed in a short piece of garden hose, complete with nozzle. He was so proud of the fireman's helmet atop his head that he insisted on wearing it instead of placing it in the compartment.

Kelvy slid the false floor back into place.

Because Kelvy was the largest, Alvin motioned him into the horse first. Kelvy climbed in and lay down. Tex Crawford was next, on top of Kelvy. Alvin then climbed in and lay face down beside Kelvy. Daphne scrambled up on top of him.

The door swung shut. The latch clicked.

"Let's go!" whispered Shoie outside. The horse groaned into motion.

Shoie and Spider had been assigned to pull the horse through the darkness. It lurched as it rolled over an uneven spot in the ground. In the total blackness inside the horse, Kelvy groaned under Tex's weight.

Alvin could feel the horse swing around a corner. It moved several feet further, then was turned once more, and stopped. According to Alvin's calculations, it must now be facing the house, just outside the gate. All the other kids should be hidden close by, in bushes and behind trees.

"All set?" whispered Shoie through a crack in the top of the horse.

"All set," said Alvin weakly, his voice muffled against the wooden floor of the box.

He heard Shoie walk up to the gate.

"Hey in there! You guys hear me? Come on out!"

A moment later Shoie whispered urgently, "The lights just came on! I'm leaving!"

Alvin's heart pounded with excitement. His breath came in weak gasps, and he could feel the Pest wiggling nervously on top of him.

By now, even Shoie would be hidden. Alvin's army crouched, armed and invisible, near the gates of Troy.

In the bleak moonlight the wooden horse peered through the fence at the enemy within.

≈17≈

Inside the Horse— the Horse Inside!

The clatter of footsteps down the porch steps . . . Pitch blackness inside the horse.

Daphne wriggled on Alvin's back. She gave a little gasp as they heard the rattle of the gate being unlocked.

Feet scuffled along the sidewalk. Alvin's hand, anchored under his left hip, began to throb.

"I'll bet it's those same kids." It was Broken Nose's voice. The wheeze of his breath. "Hey! What's this big thing on the sidewalk?"

"Stay back!" Beardface said. "Might be some kind of trick. Approach it slowly."

The muted sound of footsteps circling the horse at a distance.

Daphne whispered directly into Alvin's ear, "My belly button itches, Alvin. I've got to scratch it!"

"Don't you dare!" His whisper was low but firm. She wriggled.

The footsteps sounded closer. Another long silence. Alvin wondered anxiously what was going on. Maybe the Trojan horse wasn't such a good idea. Here they were, trapped inside the weird thing. Maybe it wasn't a good idea *at all.*

"Looks like a horse built on kids' wagons." Beardface's voice. "Goofy looking thing. Must be some kind of a joke."

"What do you think we should do, Harry? Leave it here?"

A pause. The Pest wriggled atop Alvin as she fought her silent battle with her itch.

"We've got to do something with it," Beardface said decisively. "If we leave that goofy thing standing there looking at the house, somebody might investigate. And call the cops."

"Yeah, Harry. Guess you're right."

"You *know* I'm right. I'm always right."

"Yeah. Like you said."

"We were lucky to find this crummy house for rent on a short-term basis, way out here on the edge of town where nobody has paid any attention to us. Until those kids came around. We don't want them calling attention to us now."

"You're right. Like you said."

Alvin's hand was totally asleep, and the prickles were moving up toward his elbow. He had a desperate urge to roll over.

"Well, don't just stand there. Grab that wagon tongue on the left. I'll take this other one. We'll pull the crazy thing through the gate, and then hide it behind the bushes along the wall. Nobody will see it until we're out of here."

The wagon groaned under Alvin. The horse began to lurch, and Daphne rolled back and forth across his back.

There was a pause, then the creak of the gate being opened wider. The horse rolled through the blackness again.

As the wagons left the sidewalk, the horse gave a violent lurch. It almost went over. Panic knifed through Alvin's mind. The horse swung upright again.

It shuddered to a stop.

"There," said Beardface. "Out of sight. I dunno what those kids are up to. But they can't do anything more tonight. The gate is locked, and they're on the outside."

"Yeah. On the outside. And their crazy wooden horse inside."

Footsteps scuffled off. The squeak of the porch stairs. The slam of the front door.

Daphne reached down and scratched her belly button.

≈18≈

The Gate Swings Open

An owl hooted in the distance. Alvin scarcely heard it. One ear was smashed against the rough wood of the packing crate.

"Wait!" he ordered urgently. "Freeze!" He was afraid Beardface might have second thoughts about the Trojan horse, and return to inspect it more closely. The black seconds seemed to stretch into hours.

Finally Alvin could stand it no longer. "Okay, Pest. You first. Pull the escape pin, and then push out the side of the horse."

A moment of silence. Then, "I can't!" There was panic in Daphne's voice.

"Why not?"

"The escape pin is down at my feet. And my hands are at the other end of me."

Alvin thought for a moment. "Kelvy, you goofed," he finally whispered.

"Hey!" Tex Crawford's voice had an edge of fear. "Are we locked in this thing? Can't we get out?"

"Can't we get out?" echoed the Pest.

"Sure we can. Got to use our heads." Alvin made his voice sound confident. His mind raced. "Pest, you're always bragging about your talented toes, and how good you are at yoga. Well, kick off your shoes. Then use your toes."

Daphne wriggled her feet. The suspense was agonizing. There was a soft thud as a sneaker fell to the bottom of the crate. Another thud.

"Okay, everybody," she said. "Everybody get ready to be rescued. Kelvy, tell me how to find the escape pin with my toes."

"It's up high, and right where the horse's side meets its rear end."

Squirming. Then, "I can feel it. Just a minute, you guys."

How many times in the past, thought Alvin, had his little sister rescued him from his hair-brained ideas?

"I've got it. It keeps slipping, but I'm working it loose. There!"

The side of the horse swung outward with a bang. Cool night air washed over Alvin. Moonlight flooded the horse. The Pest rolled off Alvin's back. He breathed deeply.

He tried without success to roll out of the packing crate. Half his body was paralyzed. Tex Crawford rolled across him, hit the ground and groaned his relief.

"C'mon, Alvin," demanded Kelvy, lying beside him. "Move. I can't get out until you do."

"Can't move," mumbled Alvin. "Paralyzed."

Tex's arms encircled his shoulders and lifted him out. Alvin lurched to his feet. His left shoulder drooped, and his left arm slanted uselessly down across his body.

Kelvy rolled out of the wagon and stood beside him. He lifted out the false floor, and the kids retrieved the items they had stored inside the compartment.

Four kids, free at last, stood inside the fence in the dim moonlight. Alvin patted the Trojan horse. The black hole in its side looked like a gaping wound.

"Time to make our move," he ordered. He tried to lift his arm to point to the gate, but it refused to move.

He glanced at the house. It was dark except for a single dim light upstairs. Could the men be watching from the windows? Instinctively he hunched down. The others dropped to their knees.

Alvin crawled on two knees and one hand, along the black shadows at the base of the bushes. His left arm began to tingle. *A good sign*, he thought.

Now he had to gamble. Where the wall met the big iron gate, he left the shadows and moved out into the moonlight. He wriggled along on his stomach. Suddenly the Pest's agile body shot past him. She was crouching by the gate latch when he arrived.

Alvin took a deep breath. He was almost afraid to look. If there was a padlock on the gate, he had failed; he couldn't let in his besieging army.

His breath whistled out in relief. The gate was locked with a sliding latch, a heavy steel one that was operable only from inside the fence.

He seized the handle in his good hand and pushed

upward. The latch didn't budge. By now he could lift his left arm, but he still couldn't squeeze anything with his left hand. "Help!" he whispered. "My dumb hand's numb."

Daphne's two little hands enveloped his own, and together they pushed upward. There was a rusty creak as the latch moved.

The latch suddenly sprang free, and under the weight of their bodies the big gate swung open.

"You did it, old bean!" Shoie, commanding officer of the attack force, stood just outside the open gate. Behind him in the moonlight, drawn up in orderly ranks, stood his strangely costumed army.

"The Trojan horse did it," Alvin whispered, a proud grin on his face. "Come inside, captain."

He laughed aloud at their costumes, and knew the outfit he himself was wearing was the most outlandish of all.

≈19≈

Master Plan Z

Alvin pointed toward the house, then waved his arm forward. Each of the eight figures moved noiselessly to an appointed position.

He looked down at his own costume. He laughed again, then loped toward the porch, the coil of rope in his right hand. The hand still tingled a bit, but most of the feeling had returned.

He ran up the five porch steps, and glanced over his shoulder. No one was in sight. Good.

He heard the sound of footsteps inside the house. Quickly he jumped up on the swaying porch swing and slipped a noose on one end of his rope over one of the hooks holding up the swing. He jumped down again and dashed across the porch, letting out the rope. He climbed up on the porch railing. The porch was so dark that he knew he could scarcely be seen, not even his face, which the Pest had painted black early in the evening.

Alvin Fernald took a deep breath. Now was the moment. Everything would work exactly as planned by the Magnificent Brain, or everything would turn into disaster.

"Your Girl Scout cookies are here—" he shouted toward the door, "—hand delivered to your front porch."

Nothing happened. Alvin's heart beat faster.

"GIRL SCOUT COOKIES!"

He heard the thud of footsteps inside. A light appeared behind the door. Then the door swung open.

Beardface stood silhouetted in the doorway. He took two steps forward.

Alvin bared his teeth into ugly fangs, grabbed the rope high above his head and pushed off the railing with his feet.

Beardface glanced up at the noise. A look of astonishment, then panic, crossed his face.

Swinging out of the blackness came the biggest night creature he had ever seen—a huge bat. White eyes and bared fangs gleamed wickedly in a black face, lips curled back in an evil smile, wings swung out from the hairy body as the terrible creature came diving at him through the night.

Beardface instinctively lifted his hands to shut out the horrible sight. Alvin's feet plowed into his stomach.

"OOOOOOOFFFF!"

Beardface tried to call out in horror as the huge bat sprawled across him on the porch floor, but he could only gasp.

Broken Nose lumbered through the door, tripped over a

flailing leg, and fell heavily on top of the two writhing figures.

Alvin managed to squirm out from between the two men. He scrambled down the steps on his hands and knees, then leaped to his feet. He stood there a moment, flushed with victory.

Beardface lurched to his feet. He gazed venomously down at Alvin, and suddenly seemed to recognize the costumed figure. He staggered down the steps.

Alvin fled around the corner of the house. In accordance with the master plan, Daphne was waiting.

"He's coming!" whispered Alvin as he ran past her.

Beardface, still gasping for breath, came running around the corner of the house, then stopped dead in his tracks. Facing him, legs wide apart, was the Devil himself. In this case, it was herself. There was a fiendish grin on the frightening little figure's face. Its long tail waggled back and forth as though in anticipation of some monstrous deed it was about to perpetrate. The evil face, covered with luminous paint, glowed in the dark.

The man held out his hands to fend off the weird figure, then retreated slowly around the corner. He took half a dozen steps backward. The Devil did not pursue him around the corner of the house.

"What's going on?" Broken Nose suddenly appeared behind him.

Beardface jumped. "Into the house! Lock the door! Quick!"

Broken Nose whirled and ran for the front steps. Abruptly, he stopped. Standing on the porch, shaggy arms outstretched, was a huge gorilla. The big lips were turned back in a ferocious smile. To Broken Nose the beast looked seven feet tall.

Shoie grinned inside the gorilla mask. He beat his chest with his fists, rapidly increasing the power and the strength of the blows until he was hitting himself so hard he started to cough. He took one step toward the two men below.

Broken Nose ran screaming around the house, Beard-face at his heels.

Kelvy had found the hose faucet on the side of the house. The fireman's helmet was on his head, so large that it came down around his nose and interfered with his vision. He stood in the moonlight, feet spread wide apart, hose nozzle in his hands, head tilted back so he could see.

When Broken Nose came around the corner, Kelvy opened up from five feet away. His aim was precise. The stream of water caught Broken Nose full in the face, peeling away his glasses.

The man, blinded by the stream of water, tried to reach the pint-sized fireman.

As suddenly as it started, the stream of water stopped. Broken Nose rubbed his eyes, and looked up.

And up is exactly where he continued to look. Up, and up, and up. He couldn't believe his eyes. Standing in front of him was the tallest man he had ever seen. The man was dressed in a long black cloak that covered a knobby body. A stovepipe hat disappeared up into the blackness. The tall figure seemed to undulate back and forth above him.

Inside the cloak, Seth Snyder was sweating despite the coolness of the night air. On his shoulders was his brother

Joey, and atop Joey's shoulders was Runt, only six years old. Seth had no idea how scared his little brother might be, up there high above his head.

Broken Nose stared up at the tiny little face that grinned down at him from the sky above. The face stuck out its tongue. Broken Nose took a step backward.

Meanwhile, Alvin and the Pest sneaked around the corner of the house and up the front steps. The door was wide open, and the light was on in the hallway.

Alvin had to work fast. No telling how long the other kids could keep the two men occupied. He and the Pest might be trapped inside the house at any moment.

He remembered the layout of old Mrs. Brinkley's house, and turned through the second doorway. He flipped on the light and ran across the living room to the fireplace. Above the mantel was a huge portrait of Mr. Brinkley. The stern eyes seemed to be looking directly down into Alvin's. At first they seemed to disapprove. Then, somehow, they appeared to twinkle.

The Pest dragged a chair over in front of the fireplace. Alvin crawled up on it. He tried to lift the huge, elaborately framed picture, but it was too heavy. His left hand held the frame out away from the wall, and he felt along the back of the picture with his right.

"Hurry, Alvin!" Daphne whispered urgently.

"I *am* hurrying. It doesn't do any good to say things like that when I'm already doing the best I can."

"Best you can. Sorry."

Alvin felt up one side of the frame. His fingers brushed the corner of a sheet of paper. He grabbed the corner and pulled an envelope free. "Got it!" he said triumphantly.

At that moment he heard footsteps crossing the front porch.

Alvin stepped through the doorway and glanced down the hall. Beardface came through the front door, Broken Nose at his heels. Their clothing was soaked, and Broken Nose was rubbing his eyes. Thanks to Fireman Kelvy Brown, thought Alvin.

When Beardface spotted Alvin, a look of determined hatred crossed his face. "I know you now!" he snarled at the boy in the bat's costume. "You're parading around like a bunch of monsters, but you're nothing but scared kids. Think you're pretty good at disguise, don't you? Well, I recognize you. You're the same kid who was disguised as an old man, and attacked me on the street. And you look a lot like that Girl Scout who tried to sell me cookies. I've got you now!"

The man took a slow, deliberate step forward.

The kids were trapped. "Quick! The back door!" Alvin said.

Alvin had to protect his little sister. He stood his ground while she ran from the room. A moment later he heard the rattle of a chain lock, and knew Daphne was trying to get the back door open.

"Gotcha now!"

Beardface reached out an arm. Alvin's knees went weak, and he almost fell to the floor. He heard the back door swing open, and knew that Daphne at least was safe.

Beardface lunged. He grabbed Alvin by the belt.

At that moment there was a bloodthirsty yell from the front of the house that must have echoed all the way out to Highway 64. It ended in a shriek that pierced the eardrums.

Startled, the two men glanced back over their shoulders. Leaping through the front door came a bloodthirsty Indian, naked to the waist. Long feathers stuck out of his black hair, and the savage face was crisscrossed with warpaint.

With no shirt on, Worm Wormley had been cold outside, but now that he was in action the sweat ran down his chest. He let out another bloodcurdling shriek, exactly the same kind that had won the annual Roosevelt School Yelling Contest, and swung his little brother's rubber tomahawk around his head. Broken Nose covered his ears with his hands and ran into the living room to hide.

"I'll make you pay for this," hissed Beardface. He now held Alvin securely under his arm. "You're coming along as my hostage." He dragged Alvin down the hallway toward the back door.

They were almost there when the back door opened abruptly. Standing in the doorway, as though the lord of the house, was a truly regal figure—Colonel Sanders in the flesh. The handsome old man was immaculate in a cream-colored suit. A slender bowtie fell gracefully down his shirtfront. There was a southern-style hat atop the white head, and the moustache and goatee were neatly trimmed.

Peanuts Dunkle stood behind the moustache. He forced himself to quiet his trembling knees. A benign smile spread across the Colonel's face. Peanuts carefully adjusted the cane that was hooked over his right arm.

Beardface had been momentarily taken aback, but now he recovered. "Get outta my way, kid! We're coming through!"

The Colonel brought up his hands and held out something, as though making a peace offering. It was a large cardboard tub that once had held fried chicken.

The man glanced inside the tub. Instantly he shrieked. He turned white, and let go of Alvin.

A garter snake crawled over the edge of the tub, slithered down the side, and dropped to the ground at Beardface's feet. He ran toward the front door. There, Worm Wormley let out another piercing yell, and brandished the rubber tomahawk. Beardface shot into the living room.

Colonel Sanders walked regally down the hallway carrying the tub. He stepped up to the doorway, and turned the tub upside down in the living room. Peanuts Dunkle's entire championship garter snake collection fell to the floor. The snakes slithered in all directions. Peanuts stepped back and closed the door.

Alvin, who had been watching the show, grinned through the makeup that covered his face. A fearful wail came from behind the door. It trailed off into silence.

Then the wail seemed to be echoing from outside the house. Alvin suddenly recognized the echo. It was the wail of a police siren.

Worm Wormley's bloodthirsty shrieks *had* been heard all the way out to Highway 64!

≈ **20** ≈

At Last the Riddle
Is Solved!

"Hey! Hey! Look at me! I'm a HERO!!!"
Shoie burst through the Fernald front door,
shouting as he came. Alvin, who was lying on the floor
watching television, looked up in apprehension as his
friend did a double front somersault and landed with a
crash in Dad's easy chair. The chair toppled backward, and
Shoie ended up sprawled on the floor beside Alvin.

"A hero?" asked Alvin. "What's with this hero bit?"

Three weeks had passed since Sergeant Fernald had
burst into old Mrs. Brinkley's house and rescued Beardface and Broken Nose from the disguised kids.

After Sergeant Fernald had heard the kids' excited story,
and had read Tim's letter and will, he held the two men for
questioning. Christina had promptly confirmed the de-
tails, and the men then were jailed on charges of assault,
and breaking and entering.

Peanuts Dunkle had found all but one of his prize garter snakes inside Mrs. Brinkley's living room.

Al Moser, from the *Riverton Daily Bugle*, had arrived right after the police, and had taken shots of all the kids in their disguises. The pictures had been spread across a whole page in the next evening's *Bugle*, along with a front-page news story on the kids' big adventure.

But to Alvin the adventure had not really ended. No one had been able to solve the riddle hidden in the parched yellow letter. No one had found Tim's cave, or his lost treasure.

"How come you're a big hero?" asked Alvin, looking at Shoie sprawled on the floor beside him.

"Big hero." The Pest danced into the room. She had been braiding her pigtails in her room when Shoie had made his dramatic entry.

"I *am* a hero," insisted Shoie. A big smile crossed his face. "Listen to this, you guys. *I've found the lost cave!*"

"*You've found the cave?*" Alvin and Daphne shouted in unison.

"Yep. I can lead you right to it."

"How'd you find it, old bean?" Alvin's voice was incredulous.

"Well, I got to thinking." Shoie glanced over at Alvin. "The Magnificent Brain isn't the only brain, you know," he said defensively.

"Go on, Shoie. Tell us."

"I got to thinking about those two creeks that come together and form a river that feeds into Three Crow Pond. Remember?"

"Right. The river. Go on." Alvin sat up crosslegged on

the floor. The TV program didn't matter any more.

"Well, it seemed to me there is an awful lot of water in that river from two little bitty old creeks. So this morning I went out there and started prowling around. Right above where the two creeks come together to form the river, there's a high cliff covered with underbrush and a few oak trees."

"I remember that," piped up Daphne.

"Well, for the first time in my life I climbed down the side of that cliff, hanging onto the weeds and bushes. I got about halfway down when my foot slipped, and the bush I was hanging onto pulled out of the ground. I went crashing down to the bottom of the cliff. Bonked my head on a rock real good." He rubbed the side of his head.

"Go on," Alvin said impatiently.

"Oh, Shoie, hurry up," said the Pest. "I'm just dying."

"What I found was another creek, hidden in the brush, that joins the other two. I fought my way upstream for about twenty yards, and discovered why we never knew it was there. That creek gushes out of the bottom of the cliff. It must be formed by a spring in the hillside. The creek has a lot of water in it, but it's only about twenty yards long before it flows right into the river." He stopped, then said dramatically, "Guess what else I found."

"C'mon, old bean. Stop playing games."

"In the side of the cliff, right above the spring, I found a cave."

"A cave!" whispered the Pest.

"And guess what I found inside the cave!" Shoie dropped his voice dramatically.

"What?"

"Nothing."

Alvin groaned. "Are you *sure?*"

"There's just nothing there. It's a pretty big cave that runs back into the side of the cliff. Just inside the entry is some old charred wood. Somebody must have built a fire there, long ago. There's not much light inside the cave. But I crawled inside a little ways. There's nothing there. Nothing at all."

There was a long silence in the room.

Then Daphne said in a small voice, "Take us out there, Shoie."

"It won't do any good. But I'll show you where it is."

"First let's get Christina," said Alvin, jumping to his feet. "She certainly deserves to see Tim's cave, even if there's nothing in it."

"That's a good idea," said Daphne. "You guys call Christina and tell her to come over here while I pack a picnic lunch. Let's see. I'll make some peanut butter and onion sandwiches, I'll take along some pickles, and—"

"And jelly," said Shoie firmly.

"Okay. I'll bring along some jelly, too."

"No. Peanut butter and jelly sandwiches. Not peanut butter and onion."

"Shoie, onion goes real good on peanut butter. Try it. You'll love it."

"No. I'll never try it. Peanut butter and jelly."

Alvin had been lost in thought. "We'll take along a piece of rope to help us down the cliff," he said abruptly. "And a flashlight and a shovel. Christina should bring along Tim's letter, and his will. There's something about that will . . ."

He headed toward the phone. At the doorway he turned back toward Daphne. "And jelly," he ordered. "Shoie's right. No onion."

They struggled through the bushes down the face of the cliff. Christina wore hiking boots, but they didn't keep her from slipping and sliding. Once she slipped over the edge of a rock outcropping, and would have taken a serious fall if Shoie hadn't dragged her back to safety with the rope.

At last all four figures arrived, gasping for breath, at the bottom of the cliff. There Shoie parted the bushes and pointed out a burbling stream, hidden by the undergrowth that grew along both banks.

" 'Where three streams come together,' " recited Christina, " 'you'll find a cave.' " She smiled at Shoie.

He led the way through the bushes. He hadn't gone far when he stopped. "There it is," he said, pointing up the cliff. Just above their heads was a large black hole.

Shoie scrambled up among the rocks until he was standing in the mouth of the cave. He tossed down one end of the rope. Christina grabbed it. Shoie pulled, and slowly she climbed up the hillside until she was standing beside Shoie. Alvin and the Pest quickly followed.

All four turned their backs on the bright sun and peered into the dark cavity.

"It's spooky." Daphne shivered.

Alvin turned on the flashlight. The beam cast a disc of light that danced along the walls of the cave until it vanished in the dusty interior.

"Stand ready with that shovel, Shoie," said Alvin. "Might be some critters inside you'll have to bash."

"What kind of critters?" The Pest's voice squeaked.

"I dunno," said Alvin. "Just critters. We'd better be ready."

"Okay." Shoie hefted the shovel. "You go first, old bean. You've got the flashlight."

Alvin took a deep breath. He didn't want to lead, but he couldn't see any way out. He edged into the cave with the others following. They advanced slowly until they stood in the middle of the cave.

"It's as big as our house," whispered the Pest.

"The ceiling isn't as high." For some unaccountable reason Shoie whispered too.

"And it's all rough," said Daphne. "The ceiling, I mean. It's got weird rocks hanging down."

Alvin pointed the flashlight toward the rear of the cave. The dirt floor sloped steeply upward, then leveled off to form a deep shelf across the back wall.

When Alvin stepped forward, the others followed.

He climbed up the sloping dirt floor until he came to the natural shelf. He played the flashlight across it.

"Nothing," he said. "Absolutely nothing."

When he climbed up onto the shelf to get a closer look, he hit his head on one of the rocks that hung down from the roof. He played his flashlight across the rock while he rubbed the side of his head.

"If there's nothing here," said the Pest, "then let's go outside."

It seemed a good idea to Alvin.

They stepped into the sunlight at the mouth of the cave.

Alvin flopped down and leaned against a rock. "Let's have our sandwiches," he suggested, "while we think once more about Tim's letter, and his will."

Daphne opened the paper sack she was carrying. She looked across at Christina. "What kind of sandwich would you like?"

"What's my choice, dear?"

"Peanut butter and onion, or peanut butter and jelly."

Christina thought for a moment. "Of all the days of my life, this seems the best day to take a chance. I'll have peanut butter and onion."

The Pest looked at the two boys in triumph.

They ate in silence. Alvin found himself thinking of the man who had died in the cave more than a hundred years before. As his life slowly ebbed away, Tim's thoughts had been solely of the woman he loved, and how to leave her the grubstake he had found after his long and desperate search.

Alvin licked the jelly from his fingers. "Read the part in Tim's letter about the name in his will," he said.

Christina pulled the letter from her pocket. It was wrapped in a plastic bag. Carefully she withdrew the letter and unfolded it. " 'There is a name mentioned in my will. Let this be the riddle you must solve: The name is upside down. Beneath it you will find the opals—the final gift I can bestow on you.' "

"How about letting me see the will," said Alvin. "I've almost got the answer to the puzzle. But every time the Magnificent Brain approaches it, the answer seems to disappear."

Christina handed him the will.

Alvin unfolded it. He read the entire document aloud. At the end his eyes began to shine. "I've got it!" he exclaimed. "I know the clue that Tim was trying to leave! No wonder we overlooked it!"

Christina leaned forward. "What is it, Alvin?"

"Think about it for a moment," he said crisply. "All of you. Tim says that a name will be the clue. What names are in the will?"

"We've been through all of that," Shoie said impatiently.

"Tim Martin," recited Daphne. "Ada Scheuneman. Hebron Martin. Tyler Jackson. And Benjamin Hardin."

"That's not all," said Alvin quietly. "You missed one name."

"No I didn't, Alvin. Only five people's names appeared in the will."

"I didn't say 'people.' But there's a sixth name in Tim's will."

There was a long moment of silence. Suddenly Christina said, "Ginger! Tim's horse! He willed it to Hebron!"

"Exactly."

"But what good does that do?" asked Shoie. "I mean, the name of a horse doesn't tell us anything."

"I think it does." Alvin rubbed his head where he had hit it on the rock. "I think it tells us exactly where the opals are buried. Come on. Bring the shovel."

Alvin led the way back through the cave. As he climbed up the sloping floor he began to run. He stopped in front of the big, deep shelf. The others crowded around. Alvin pointed the flashlight at the rock that had caught the side of his head.

The rock cast a huge shadow on the back wall of the cave,

a shadow that seemed to dance as the flashlight trembled in Alvin's excited hands.

Christina said, "It's a horse. It's the shadow of a horse's head."

"A horse's head hanging upside down from the roof of the cave!" exclaimed the Pest.

"The nose is hanging downward, just like it was pointing at something," said Shoie.

"And I'll bet it's pointing at Tim's treasure," said Alvin, a note of triumph in his voice. " 'The name is upside down.' Hand me the shovel, old man."

He climbed up until he could reach the loose dirt below the odd-shaped rock. Slowly he began moving the dirt to one side. It was hard going. The sweat began running down his cheeks.

"Let me dig for a while," offered Shoie.

"Not on your life. I *know* that treasure is here, and I'm going to find it."

He dug deeper and deeper. Nothing.

For the first time, Alvin began having doubts. When the shovel struck a hard object, his heart leaped. It was only a rock.

Shoie was holding the flashlight. Alvin had just tossed a shovelful of dirt to one side, when Shoie exclaimed, "Wait, old man! There's something there!"

Alvin looked at the pile of dirt. Half lost in it was a leather lace. He pulled at the lace and watched in excitement as a dusty pouch appeared. It was a pouch buried by a dying man, protected for more than a hundred years by the dry dust of the cave.

Alvin dropped the shovel and cradled the pouch to his

chest, as though it was something still alive after all those years. In a sense, it was.

"Come on. Let's take it out into the sunlight."

Outside, in the mouth of the cave, he took his handkerchief from his pocket and spread it carefully on the ground. The others squatted around.

His fingers shook as he pulled at the leather lacing. He tilted the pouch.

Out tumbled a dozen beautiful milky-white stones. He tilted the bag still more. A river of stones fell onto the handkerchief. As they caught the sunlight they seemed to come alive. A rainbow of colors flashed from deep inside the stones.

"Wow!" exclaimed Shoie.

"Beautiful!" whispered the Pest.

"BINGOOOOO!" shouted Alvin in triumph.

He looked across at Christina. Tears flowed down her cheeks.

≈21≈

Master of a Thousand Disguises

By midafternoon, tired but excited, they were back in Riverton. Christina suggested that they go straight to the police station and report the finding of the treasure. "There may be legal aspects we know nothing about," she observed.

Sergeant Fernald shared their excitement.

"Alvin was the one who did it," explained Christina. "He solved the riddle, and led us straight to the opals."

"Aw, c'mon," said Alvin. "It was Shoie who found the cave. And—and it was the Pest who got us out of the Trojan horse with her toes."

Al Moser came bustling into the room and took his camera out of its case. "Here we go again, Alvin," he said. "Seems like for one reason or another I find myself taking pictures of you every few days. No disguises this time? Just as well. All of you kids gather around Christina and look at the opals."

Flash after flash. The sensation of having his picture taken was nothing new to Alvin. How many times, in triumph or in trouble, had he been in front of Mr. Moser's lens?

Finally the camera was back in the case. The photographer became a reporter. Mr. Moser pulled a notebook from his pocket, took a pencil from behind his ear, and said, "Just a few questions."

Twenty minutes later Alvin finished the story. "We poured all those opals out on my handkerchief. They were beautiful."

"Quite an adventure," said Mr. Moser. "And now it's over. What are your thoughts right now, Alvin?"

Alvin dropped his eyes to the floor. He began tugging at his right earlobe. "Most of all, I guess I wish Tim was here to claim his grubstake."

Mr. Moser cleared his throat. "And how about you, Christina? A hundred years and more ago a dying man wrote a last will leaving those gems to his fiancée. You are the most direct descendant, so presumably the courts will decide that the opals are yours. What will you do with them?"

A smile crossed Christina's face. "I'm going to select the four biggest and most valuable opals. I'll sell three of them and divide the money between Alvin, Shoie, and Daphne."

"And what will you do with the fourth opal?"

"I'll have it mounted in gold. I'll have it hung from a gold chain. I'll give it to Mrs. Fernald for safekeeping. She is to present it to Daphne on the morning of her wedding day. Perhaps it will remind her of a love story that happened many, many years ago."

Alvin looked down at his little sister. There were tears in her eyes.

He cleared a lump that had appeared in his own throat. *Sentimental slob*, he thought.

"Come on, old man," he said to Shoie. "Let's go check out the costumes at the Summer Theater. Maybe we can buy some of them with our share of the money from the opals. Maybe we can revive the Summer Theater, and make it into a Children's Theater. Maybe we can write our own plays, and produce them ourselves. Maybe we can—"

Alvin Fernald, Master of a Thousand Disguises, waved and headed out the door.